# ENDANGERED LANGUAGES

T0120485

**The MIT Press Essential Knowledge Series**

A complete list of books in this series can be found online at
https://mitpress.mit.edu/books/series/mit-press-essential-knowledge-series.

# ENDANGERED LANGUAGES

## EVANGELIA ADAMOU

The MIT Press | Cambridge, Massachusetts | London, England

The MIT Press would like to thank the anonymous peer reviewers who provided comments on drafts of this book. The generous work of academic experts is essential for establishing the authority and quality of our publications. We acknowledge with gratitude the contributions of these otherwise uncredited readers.

This book was set in Chaparral Pro by New Best-set Typesetters Ltd. Printed and bound in the United States of America.

Library of Congress Cataloging-in-Publication Data

Names: Adamou, Evangelia, author.
Title: Endangered languages / Evangelia Adamou.
Description: Cambridge, Massachusetts : The MIT Press, 2024. | Series: The MIT Press essential knowledge series | Includes bibliographical references and index.
Identifiers: LCCN 2023032401 (print) | LCCN 2023032402 (ebook) | ISBN 9780262548700 (paperback) | ISBN 9780262379199 (epub) | ISBN 9780262379182 (pdf)
Subjects: LCSH: Endangered languages.
Classification: LCC P40.5.E53 A33 2024 (print) | LCC P40.5.E53 (ebook) | DDC 306.44—dc23/eng/20231026
LC record available at https://lccn.loc.gov/2023032401
LC ebook record available at https://lccn.loc.gov/2023032402

10  9  8  7  6  5  4  3  2  1

In memory of my father, Apostolos Adamos
1936–2022

# CONTENTS

# SERIES FOREWORD

The MIT Press Essential Knowledge series offers accessible, concise, beautifully produced pocket-size books on topics of current interest. Written by leading thinkers, the books in this series deliver expert overviews of subjects that range from the cultural and the historical to the scientific and the technical.

In today's era of instant information gratification, we have ready access to opinions, rationalizations, and superficial descriptions. Much harder to come by is the foundational knowledge that informs a principled understanding of the world. Essential Knowledge books fill that need. Synthesizing specialized subject matter for nonspecialists and engaging critical topics through fundamentals, each of these compact volumes offers readers a point of access to complex ideas.

As a professional linguist, my job is to study the mechanics of languages. More specifically, I'm the kind of linguist who studies the mechanics of endangered languages.

But my interest in endangered languages is also personal. I grew up in Greece in the 1970s. Everyone around me used Modern Greek: we spoke Greek at home, Greek at school, Greek with friends, Greek in the city market, and Greek on the radio and TV. Greek was everywhere.

Yet something linguistically exciting happened whenever I visited my grandparents' village, just a thirty-minute drive from the city of Thessaloniki, where my family and I lived. Rushing around to make lunch, my mother and grandmother sometimes used a language that they never used to talk to me, creating their own mother-daughter bubble.

I quickly realized that some of the loving or teasing words my grandparents used with me were unknown to my schoolfellows. That was a "eureka" moment for me: I wrote down a minidictionary of my essential words and phrases, like how to ask my grandmother to prepare eggs in tomato sauce for dinner. The dictionary has since been lost, but I have been able to make up for the loss.

When I moved to France for my doctoral studies, I learned about minoritized languages in France and Europe. This new knowledge opened avenues of understanding about the place I came from. So when I finished my PhD and became a mother, I decided to look deeper into my family's heritage. I went back to my grandparents' village, and under their guidance, talked to their friends, asked questions, and recorded them, and finally had the solution to my childhood mystery: what the people in the village called *Nashta*, "our language," is a Balkan Slavic variety.

I read books, and more books, and learned that Slavic speakers settled in the village in the sixth century. We know that because there are a couple of references in historical documents from the Byzantine era. My family and others in the village are traditionally Christian Orthodox and identify as Greeks. I mention religion here because religious affiliation—not language—was key during the Ottoman Empire. So when my family's village became part of the Greek state in 1912–1913, their religious identity aligned with the core identity of the newly founded nation-state. All that remained to be done was to shift from Nashta to Modern Greek. The shift was complete within a couple of generations, with the community gaining access to formal schooling (unsurprisingly, in Greek only) and transitioning from a predominantly farming society to a blue- and white-collar one.

Reconnecting with my family's roots and language was important to me, and I like to think that my research on Nashta gave joy to everyone involved in the project. My grandparents now rest in peace, the recordings are securely archived and curated parts can be consulted online, and I have published a grammar of Nashta and other scholarly work in their honor.

When I joined the French National Centre for Scientific Research (CNRS) as a tenured researcher, I was eager to learn more about the experiences of other communities across the world. I collaborated with some extraordinary people who taught me Pomak (a Slavic language spoken in Greece by Muslim communities) and Romani (an Indic language spoken throughout Europe and the Americas by the Roma people). I also had the immense privilege of contributing to a language documentation program on Ixcatec (Xhwani), an Otomanguean language spoken in Mexico by less than ten people, most of them being, at the time, seventy-five or older.

Even though I bring my professional and personal experience to this book, it goes beyond myself and my own community's experience. Each chapter therefore starts with a quote highlighting remarkable voices on language reclamation and language justice from around the world. What all of these inspirational people agree on is that now is the time to support communities in their journey to reclaim their languages.

**Writing Conventions**

In this book, I follow the Linguistic Society of America and American Psychological Association guidelines for reducing bias.

Languages, language groupings, and group names are capitalized. As such, I capitalize the names *Indigenous*, *Aboriginal*, and *Creoles*, and use specific names for languages and groups when appropriate. I do not capitalize *pidgins* and *sign languages* as these terms do not refer to related language groupings but instead types of languages. I only capitalize these terms when they form part of a specific language name.

I capitalize *Deaf* to honor the preference of individuals who culturally identify as Deaf. When I am not referring specifically to signers (users of sign languages) or speakers (users of spoken languages), I use the generic terms *language user* and *language community*.

As much as I try to use the preferred language and group names of each community, I rely primarily on the names used in the sources I cite. Variations throughout the book reflect different varieties and spellings.

I opted for the bilingual name Aotearoa New Zealand, which is increasingly being used in official and academic contexts to reflect the country's history. Note, however, that Aotearoa is the name currently used in te reo Māori, but was initially used to refer solely to the North Island. The full name is Aotearoa me Te Waipounamu, which includes a reference to the South Island.

I use gender-neutral language and the singular gender-neutral third-person pronouns *they/their*.

# INTRODUCTION

### What We Mean When We Talk about Endangered Languages

The Myaamia language is not an extinct language, even though it was labeled an extinct language 20-some years ago. It begs the question—do these languages really go extinct?

—Daryl Baldwin, quoted in "Myaamia Center and Language Revitalization" by Kristi Eaton

**What Is a Language?**

Languages are a brilliant way for humans to communicate and achieve things together. As you read these words, somewhere in the world, a parent uses language to teach their child to ride a bicycle, teens use language playfully at a party, a surgeon and their team use technical language as they perform a lifesaving surgery, and millions use language on social media to argue about social media.

Yet languages are much more than sophisticated communication and argumentation tools. Languages express belonging to a community, land, and religion. Languages trigger emotions and memories. Languages are intertwined with art, law, and all kinds of knowledge, from foundational stories about how humans came into being to which herbs soothe a sore throat.

Baby humans learn whatever languages are used around them, exploiting their impressive memory skills, an associative learning capacity that helps them associate different events and joint attention with their caregivers as they explore the world around them. This is a unique way of learning and using language that computers cannot truly imitate beyond processing large amounts of language data and applying rules.[1]

How about animals? Many animals are social and communicate with one another in ways that resemble human languages. For instance, dolphins rely on whistles and even use unique signature whistles corresponding to distinct names for one another like we do.[2] Nonetheless, researchers agree that nonhuman communication is significantly different from human language in that humans can talk about things that are not in the here and now, elaborate extensively on our thoughts, and adjust our speech to a variety of audiences.

Distinctions between human languages and animal communication are reflected in the differences between the human brain and the brains of other species. While the human brain and that of nonhuman primates are similar in many ways, the parts of the human brain where languages are rooted are more robust.[3]

In addition, researchers have discovered that there is considerable behavioral, neural, and genetic similarity between auditory-vocal learning in human infants and songbirds, both relying on prosody and rhythm.[4] Even though the brain of birds is tiny, it contains similar numbers of neurons to the much bigger brain of mammals; it's just packaged in a denser form.[5]

Scientists are beginning to understand that a wide network of regions of the human brain is involved in language production and comprehension. They already knew of the importance of two areas: Broca's area, which is primarily associated with language production and located near the motor cortex, which controls language-related muscles such as the muscles of the face, mouth, and vocal cords; and Wernicke's area, which is mainly associated with language comprehension and located near the auditory cortex, which allows us to hear. These areas are roughly the same across speakers of different languages, yet each speaker's language network differs as it is constantly shaped by language experience.[6]

Sign languages, the languages used by Deaf people, are processed in similar areas in the brain and differ from spoken languages only to the extent that they draw more heavily on the visual modality (signers use codified manual signs together with facial expressions, head positions, and body postures).[7]

Given that languages are anchored in the human brain and performed through social interaction, linguists often draw the conclusion that when the last speaker or signer of a language dies, then the language has also died.

But languages can be written and read too—that is, if there are written records and the code of the script has been cracked. While only 60 percent of the world's languages are written, acquisition of literacy connects preexisting parts of the brain for language and vision.[8] It follows that any language can be written when its users need to write it down or have been exposed to other written languages. And this is what people frequently do when they learn to read and write in one language: they use the same script to write in another language even when this language is not officially written and taught at school.

Writing doesn't prevent a language from ceasing to be used. Sumerian, for example, the language of a powerful empire that existed four thousand years ago in Mesopotamia, is no longer spoken today. Nonetheless, writing offers the extraordinary possibility to access texts in a language even after its users have died. Sumerian was put into writing, allowing us to witness traces of its actuality.

Being able to access any kind of documentation in a language that is no longer performed here and now offers the opportunity to reclaim that language. This is the reason why language practitioners from communities where most language keepers have recently passed away advise the use of the terms *dormant*, *sleeping*, *awakening*, or *in reclamation* rather than *extinct*, or even worse, *dead*, indicating that there is a possibility of reawakening and reclaiming their language.[9]

Modern Hebrew illustrates such successful reawakening. It now has millions of language users even though it had been restricted to use in religious contexts for centuries.

We should therefore probably favor the term dormant since most languages can be reclaimed by a language community even centuries later.

### How Many Languages Are Used around the World?

Let's now look at some numbers. Take a moment to guess how many languages are used across the globe. Tip: it's in the thousands. To see if your guess was close, keep reading!

To the best of our knowledge, there are currently seven thousand languages.[10]

Nearly seven thousand languages for eight billion people. Yet the distribution of speakers and signers for each language is uneven. Most of the languages are used by a tiny portion of the world's population: just a few million people currently speak more than 90 percent of all languages. In other words, a few superlanguages run the world, with more than a hundred million speakers each.

English is used by millions of speakers as a first or second language, like I do in this book to share ideas with people around the world. Spanish is spoken all over Latin America in addition to Spain; Mandarin Chinese is spoken by nearly a billion people; and Arabic, Hindi, Bengali, Portuguese, Russian, and Japanese are used daily by millions of speakers.

Knowing this, can you guess how many languages are at risk of no longer having any language users soon? Since you are reading this book, you probably know that there are plenty. Take a guess at a percentage. Is it closer to 10 or 90 percent of all languages?

According to Glottolog, 58 percent of languages are endangered.[11] In numbers, this represents about four thousand languages. This is a shockingly high figure. When we break down this amount, we realize that roughly 10 percent of languages have fewer than ten language keepers. These are the languages that are the most likely to become dormant in the coming years. The pace is slower than initially thought: careful estimates establish that one language stops being used every three months, not every two weeks.[12] This means that in the next hundred years, if nothing changes, four hundred more languages will become dormant.

According to Glottolog,
58 percent of languages
are endangered.

Numbers can be difficult to fully grasp so I have created a figure for visualization (figure 1). The endangered languages are at the top of the box, and the safe languages are at the bottom.

How does it feel to know that more than half of humanity's languages are in danger? Most of us can't immediately grasp why such a drop in the number of human languages is bad news.

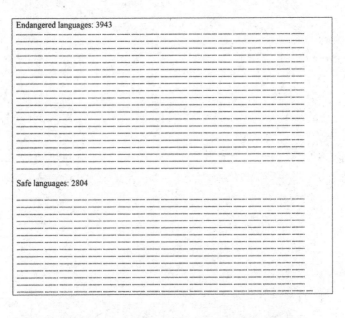

**Figure 1** Representation of endangered and safe languages based on Glottolog's Agglomerated Endangerment Status. *Source*: Harald Hammarström et al., *Glottolog* 4.7 (Leipzig: Max Planck Institute for Evolutionary Biology, 2022), https://doi.org/10.5281/zenodo.7398962.

So let's try this. I'd like you to briefly imagine that the language that you learned as a child is no longer used or known by anyone else in the world. All the emotions you feel when you use the language are now surfacing along with the memory of your caregivers, family members, teachers, friends, and foes. All of these emotions, dreams, jokes, and knowledge are at risk of being lost forever. You may even start feeling upset to know that your language is reduced to a simple figure on a language endangerment list. Your language is more than a number.

## How Are Languages Counted?

"How are languages counted" can be broken down into three different questions: "How do we assign language-hood?" "How do we decide that Language A is different from Language B?" and "Who gets to name languages?" Let's answer them each in turn.

### How Do We Assign Languagehood?

Recall that we have loosely defined languages as a means of communication between humans. Does this mean that whistled languages are languages like English? What about pidgins?

Some linguists argue that whistled languages and pidgins are like other languages since they allow humans to communicate. Others consider that these languages are restricted to specific communication contexts and should therefore be termed differently, as *registers*.

For example, whistled languages are developed for long-distance communication among shepherds or hunters in environments like the mountains and dense forests where they can't have their voices easily heard.[13] A whistle can be heard ten times farther than the human voice and blends in better with nonhuman communication.

Pidgins are likewise typically restricted to communication in trade. They arise in multilingual contexts where people don't share a common language. For instance, Bazaar Malay is a pidgin that has been used for many centuries in Southeast Asia among Chinese, Arab, Javanese, and Europeans as they trade much-valued spices like cloves, pepper, and cinnamon.[14] In linguistic terms, pidgins result from the combination of the lexicon of the foreign traders' languages with the grammars of the local languages.

Which languages get assigned languagehood is also a matter of ideology. For example, Creoles, the languages developed in the adverse conditions of enslavement and racial segregation on plantations, have long been denied consideration as full-fledged languages. Michel DeGraff, Massachusetts Institute of Technology linguist and speaker of Kreyòl (Haitian Creole), explains that these negative language ideologies were based on the racial theories of the times, when scholars considered that the enslaved Africans were incapable of learning the presumed "advanced" western European languages.[15] Against this view, current research highlights the complex multilingualism that abounded in the colonies, giving rise to Creoles through a combination of the lexicon of the colonizers' languages (like English, Spanish, French, Dutch, and Portuguese) and the grammar and phonology of a variety of African languages.

Sign languages were also long denied languagehood and instead considered a mere collection of gestures, without any grammatical structure or access to abstract concepts.[16] We know today that there is a variety of sign languages ranging from individual home sign languages created by D/deaf children born into hearing families that don't know a sign language, to traditional sign languages created and used within Indigenous and rural communities, and to the bigger urban, national, and international sign languages that are often used in formal education.

Although Creoles and sign languages are now recognized as full-fledged languages, there is still progress to be made to shift the negative language ideologies of the past and acknowledge the linguistic rights of their speakers and signers.

## How Do We Decide That Language A Is Different from Language B?

One might think that the answer to this question is straightforward. After all, you are reading these words that

I wrote in the English language for you to read. If I switch to ελληνικά, για παράδειγμα, you will no longer know what I'm saying; the expression "it's all Greek to me" is apt as I indeed switched to Modern Greek, my first language.

To tell two languages apart, linguists conduct a similar task: they bring together two language users and see whether they can communicate, with each of them using their own language. While users of Languages A and B may successfully go through the greetings part of a conversation, they may get stuck when it comes to more complex issues, such as technical instructions or simply sharing their life stories. We will probably decide that Languages A and B are indeed different since they do not allow users to fully communicate with one another.

While this method works well to tell apart languages that have been spoken for centuries in distant geographic areas, it becomes more complicated to tell languages apart that have at some point in their history been spoken by populations living in proximity. We have seen, for example, that English is one of the languages in the world that has the greatest number of speakers, both as a first and second language (or third, fourth, etc.). So do all English speakers speak the same English language? Aren't there instead many Englishes?

This is where the different status and extent of use of a language enters the equation of interintelligibility. In fact, chances are that speakers of English as spoken in a small rural community will better understand English speakers in the national media. The opposite is rarer. These are no longer purely linguistic criteria (how many words and how much of the grammar are similar for successful communication to happen) but rather are known as sociolinguistic criteria: What is the power imbalance between two languages? As the famous saying goes, "A language is a dialect with an army and a navy."[17]

Thus it is often difficult to decide whether a language can be granted the coveted status of language or will instead be referred to as a dialect. This means that even though you may not be able to communicate with a speaker of an English dialect that you are not familiar with, this dialect will not automatically be upgraded to language status.

Sometimes, even today, people refer to all the languages spoken in their country as dialects, including when these are officially recognized languages. In France, I have heard people refer to Breton, Basque, and the numerous languages of New Caledonia and French Guiana as dialects. In Mexico, people also refer to Indigenous languages as dialects. These are all languages with their own set of dialects.

Given the heavy ideological load obscuring the use of these terms, linguists are increasingly recommending the universal use of the term *language* as it carries no value judgment. Dialect can be used when the distinction is made by a community or government body.[18]

To understand the proximity of two languages, or a language and dialect in an asymmetrical power relation, linguists have developed tools that allow them to group languages into language families and subgroupings known as language branches. The metaphor used is one of genealogical trees, where certain languages share a common ancestor. This is of course a highly idealized tree, and the common ancestor is typically not attested.

In fact, chances are there were multiple groups of speakers at the time of the ancestor language, and within these groups of speakers there was significant language variation. We can safely say this because we now know that variation is inherent to language: some language users use language slightly differently from other language users in a language community and can change their own way of using language across their life span.

For instance, teenagers typically speak differently from older adults as they experiment with their identity. Also, if a group's activities are strongly divided along gender lines, then each subgroup may develop slightly different ways of speaking, sometimes giving rise to distinct *genderlects* (more about this topic in chapter 6).

It is important to bear in mind that variation is inherent to language, and this is what brings about language change and in some cases the split of Language A into two languages: Language B and Language C. With time, Languages B and C may grow further apart.

When Languages B and C have grown apart, users of Language B may want to claim their independence. Users of Language C may refuse to accept that based on their shared ancestor, Language A.

This can give rise to the kind of tensions seen around the status of Macedonian with respect to Bulgarian, two closely related South Slavic languages spoken in the Balkans. Until 2022, Bulgaria, a member state of the European Union, had opposed the accession of the state of North Macedonia to the European Union, demanding the removal of any mention of the Macedonian language from official documents. From the Bulgarian perspective, Macedonian is just a dialect of Bulgarian. From the Macedonian perspective, Macedonians should have the right to their own national language. Nashta, the southernmost Slavic variety of my ancestors spoken in Greece, has been caught up in this controversy as it is claimed by these two neighboring national languages. This is the reason why it is a politically sensitive topic in Greece. More will be said about nation-states, national languages, and the (non)recognition of minoritized languages in chapter 5.

Now what about when people decide to consistently speak two languages at once? Bilinguals sometimes like to use two languages in a single conversation, and even within a single sentence. In the United States, for example, some speakers alternate between Spanish and English, leading critics to consider that they don't know how to speak either properly. Yet this way of switching from one language to another is not a sign of deficiency of some sort but signals instead a unique mixed identity.

In rare cases, such bilingual practices can form new *mixed languages*. The Glottolog database identifies ten such independent mixed languages, but this low number may be because we have only started identifying mixed languages. Linguists distinguish two types of mixed languages: those that combine the grammar of one language with the lexicon of another, and those that combine the nouns of one language with the verbs of another.

For instance, Gurindji Kriol, a mixed language spoken in the Victoria River district of northern Australia, combines nouns and their grammar from Gurindji as well as verbs and their grammar from Kriol (i.e., an English-based Creole that is currently used by thousands of Aboriginal people).[19] In the 1970s, as the Gurindji community was shifting from its ancestral Gurindji language to Kriol, an important political movement halted the process. This led to the emergence of this new language, Gurindji Kriol, reflecting the new Gurindji identity. Using a unique language name like Gurindji Kriol is one way of explicitly acknowledging the existence of a language.

### Who Gets to Name Languages?

In everyday life, we rely on handy labels as proxies for languages. But who has the authority to assign these labels?

Linguists note that language names are haphazard tags that the powerful have given to languages, like when they outline countries on a map with arbitrary borders after a war.

Language names are often given by outsiders, in their own language. Sometimes language names given by outsiders can be derogatory. For example, I studied an Otomanguean language spoken in the state of Oaxaca, Mexico, that is known as Chocho, from the Spanish verb *chochear*, which means to "babble like a senile person." Even though this language name has been common practice, speakers and community members are now reclaiming their group's internal language names, meaning "our language," Ngigua and Ngiba (with variation depending on the variety spoken).[20]

Language names used by the speakers themselves often simply mean "our language" as uttered in the language itself; this is the case for Nashta, a Slavic variety that has been spoken in my maternal grandmother's community in Greece since the sixth century. Nashta literally means "ours." Some think that this is a political strategy because Slavic varieties do not have official status in Greece. Yet Slavic speakers in Italy use the same root to form the name of their language (Na Nashu), even though their language is officially recognized.

Indeed, referring to one's language as *our language* is common throughout the world and independent of the language's status. When I started working on the Oto-manguean language of Mexico known as Ixcatec, a name based on the Nahuatl word for "cotton," I realized that the language's name in Ixcatec itself is *xhwani*, meaning "our language" (the name is pronounced *sh$^h$wa$^2$ni$^3$*, with a strong puff of air after *sh* and a middle lexical tone for the first syllable followed by a low lexical tone for the second).

Language names frequently change. Another illustration of speaker-initiated language name change is that of the previously called Serbo-Croatian language. Following the Yugoslav Wars of the 1990s and the formation of separate states, Serbo-Croatian has given way to the Bosnian, Croatian, Montenegrin, and Serbian languages (presented here in alphabetical order). Are these languages similar? Yes, they are. Some linguists even use the abbreviation BCMS to stress the linguistic similarity of these languages. Do people who have experienced war want to name their language differently? Yes, they do, and language experts should be ready to acknowledge this.

Ultimately, as the scholars of applied linguistics Sin-free Makoni, Cristine Severo, and Ashraf Abdelhay argue, the concept and activity of counting and naming languages are strongly related to modern nation-state building, or-thographic literacy, and language standardization—aspects that I discuss in more detail in chapters 3 and 5.[21]

Nevertheless, in a (post)positivist frame, linguists strive to classify, name, and count the languages of the world in the most transparent way possible. They listen to what language communities prefer as their language name and clearly mention any alternate names. At the same time, native language names can be similar or overlap, so specialists look for ways to better organize the identification of all languages. To this end, unique identifiers have been created, starting with the ISO 693–3 codes proposed by the Protestant missionary organization Summer Institute of Linguistics.[22] Similarly, academics at Glottolog have been using language codes by combining letters and numbers; for instance, the identifier aaril1239 is used for the Aari language.

## How Are Endangered Languages Counted?

Let's now discover how endangered languages are counted. In this book, I chose to showcase Glottolog's estimates of endangered languages because they combine all available sources, and are up to date and freely available online. But when we look at the original sources, we realize there are significant differences. For instance, according to estimates by the United Nations Educational, Scientific, and Cultural Organization (UNESCO), 83 percent of languages would be endangered.[23] In turn, the Catalogue of Endangered Languages estimates that roughly 45.6 percent of languages are endangered.[24] Why are there such important differences?

First, estimates vary because of the criteria used to decide what counts as a language, as we have seen in the previous section. Second, estimates vary because of the criteria used to decide what counts as endangered.

To capture differences in language usage, researchers, and institutions like UNESCO have developed endangerment scales. A comprehensive proposal is that of the Language Endangerment Index elaborated by the Catalogue of Endangered Languages researchers.[25] This index combines scores ranging from zero (all good) to five (it's time to act) using four criteria: intergenerational transmission, number of speakers and signers, speaker and signer number trends, and domains of use.

- Intergenerational transmission

Intergenerational transmission is hugely important and can be summarized as follows: the more children use a language and the longer they keep using it throughout their life, the better.

For intergenerational transmission, specialists allot five points to a language when there are only a few older adult users; four when the language is used by many members of the generation of grandparents; three when in addition to the grandparental generation, some younger adults use the language; two when most young adults use the language; one when children use the language; and zero when all members of a language community, irrespective of their age, use the language. These scores are then multiplied by two as this criterion is important.

- Number of language users

    Another significant criterion is to know how large the community of speakers and signers is. Small language communities are vulnerable to natural disasters (particularly relevant in a time of climate breakdown), wars, and of course pandemics (like the global COVID-19 pandemic that started in 2020).

    To assess the status of a language, specialists allot five points when there are fewer than ten speakers and signers; four when there are up to a hundred speakers and signers; three when there are up to a thousand speakers and signers; two when there are up to ten thousand speakers and signers; one when there are up to a hundred thousand speakers and signers; and zero when there are more than a hundred thousand speakers and signers.

- Language user number trends

    Language user number trends is a criterion that aims to capture the rates of speakers and signers within a language community. For instance, there might be some localities where the language is used by everyone in the community, but in other localities the language is used by only a small number of people. This may hint at an ongoing language shift that may sooner or later generalize to all communities.

For this criterion, specialists allot five points when a small percentage of the community uses the language; four when less than half the community members use the language and the trend is toward language shift; three when half the community members use the language and there is no significant ongoing decrease; two when a majority of community members uses the language yet the numbers are slowly decreasing; one when most community members use the language and speaker or signer numbers are slowly decreasing; and zero when everyone uses the language and the number of speakers and signers is either stable or increasing.

- Domains of use

    The domains in which a language is used is a classic criterion in the study of endangered languages. It aims to describe the opportunities for speakers and signers to use their language.

    While it is lovely to use a language at home, in twenty-first-century societies this is often considered too restricted. If you cannot use your language at work, to study, to surf on the internet, and so on, the fear is that eventually the imbalance will become too great and speakers will more easily recall the words and grammar of the language they use more frequently. This then triggers a vicious circle where the less available a language becomes in the mind, the less likely people are to use it.

At the same time, home is the place where language is strongly connected to emotions. Language use at home is also rich, ranging from playing with our kids to discussing politics when family comes to visit.

For this criterion, specialists allot five points when the language is limited to ceremonies, prayers, songs, and some domestic activities; four when the language is mainly used at home along with other languages; three when the language is mainly used at home, but is the only language used; two when the language is used at home as well as in some nonofficial domains; one when the language is used in most domains except the official ones; and zero when the language is used in most domains, including official ones such as in government, media, and education.

The sum of the scores for the above criteria provide an overall figure: the higher it is, the more endangered the language is in comparison to others. The score allows researchers to classify a language on a scale of endangerment that ranges from critically endangered through severely endangered, endangered, threatened, vulnerable, at risk, and safe (these terms can vary depending on various endangerment scales).

The position of a language on the endangerment scale aims to inform communities and decision-makers in language documentation and language revitalization. At the same time, endangerment scales are criticized by practitioners for reducing language communities to rankings and fostering a logic of triage when resources are allocated. While it is painful to assign a score to a language, institutions consider that it is useful to zoom out and obtain an understanding of what the global situation is and thus inform language policies. Alternative suggestions include the replacement of endangerment scales by actions focusing on vitality and sustainability.[26]

**Key Takeaways**

• There are about seven thousand languages used by eight billion people across the globe. Fifty-eight percent of these languages are endangered.

• One language becomes dormant every three months.

• Endangered languages are languages, not dialects. In fact, endangered languages generally have different dialects.

• Two languages are different when their users cannot communicate with one another while using their language. But two languages are also different when their users consider them to be different for cultural and historical reasons.

- Language names are sometimes given by outsiders and can be derogatory. Some language groups contest these names and promote the language name as pronounced in their own language, often meaning "our language."

- To establish whether a language is endangered, researchers and institutions assess the vitality of intergenerational transmission, number of speakers and signers, speaker and signer number trends, and domains in which the language is used.

# WHERE ARE ENDANGERED LANGUAGES FOUND?

*Ngada marraaju kilwanmaruthu ngijinju dulku*—"I want to show you all my country."

—Mirdidingkingathi Juwarnda Sally Gabori, quoted in "Sally Gabori" by Elli Walsh

Endangered languages can be found everywhere in the world; 180 out of 193 member states of the United Nations host at least one endangered language. A word of caution: such accounts generally respect the political status quo in each country (recall the discussion we had about what counts as a language), and the number of endangered languages around the world is certainly much higher.

In what follows, I am using the term *Indigenous* to refer to people and languages. What does *Indigenous* mean? Rather than offering a strict definition, the United Nations proposes a human rights approach according to which any group has the right to self-identify as Indigenous. In general, the term *Indigenous* refers to people who inhabited a territory before the arrival of settlers; this is also captured by the term *First Nations*. The term *Aboriginal*—from Latin, meaning "original inhabitants"—is used more specifically to refer to the Indigenous Peoples of Australia, though some authors are increasingly using the terms *Indigenous* and *First Nations*.

Please keep in mind, however, that Indigenous people themselves did not need to self-identify as such prior to European colonization. Rather, *Indigenous* is a term that lumps together a great variety of linguistically and culturally diverse groups with different histories.

I will therefore try, whenever possible, to refer to specific groups and languages by their names.

Let's now zoom in on the six macro areas: Africa, Eurasia, Australia, Oceania, North America and Mesoamerica, and South America. All language names, spellings, and numbers are from the Glottolog database, and are sometimes rounded for ease of reading.[1]

There are names of languages and language families that you will most likely encounter for the first time. That's intentional: speakers and signers of endangered languages want us to know these names. You can take your time and pronounce the language names to get a grasp of their specific sound combinations. Of course, I cannot include all four thousand names of endangered languages in

Rather, *Indigenous* is a term that lumps together a great variety of linguistically and culturally diverse groups with different histories.

this book. If you want to discover more languages, please visit Glottolog's website. We will see in the next chapters that you can also listen to some of the world's endangered languages and watch videos online.

I refer to the current dating of language families to show readers that most languages, not just those with extensive written records, have been used for centuries. Readers should keep in mind, though, that these estimates are subject to controversy.

Also, although I provide some historical background for each area, their past is long and complex, and I encourage interested readers to consult the available sources to learn more.

## Africa

Let's start with Africa, where our common ancestor, Homo sapiens, evolved 200,000 years ago.[2]

At present, almost one-third of the world's languages are to be found on the African continent, or more than 2,000 languages.

**Figure 2** Distribution of endangered languages across the world. White encodes loss, light gray hues denote great danger, dark gray denotes risk, and the darkest hues denote no danger. *Source*: Harald Hammarström et al., *Glottolog* 4.7 (Leipzig: Max Planck Institute for Evolutionary Biology, 2022), https://doi.org/10.5281/zenodo.7398962.

Africa is the homeland of two large language families, Atlantic-Congo in the south and Afro-Asiatic in the north, along with other smaller families throughout the continent.

The largest language family is Atlantic-Congo, comprising 1,300 languages spoken by some 600 million people. The Bantu language group alone has over 240 million speakers. Who are the Bantu people and how did they come to form such a large group of speakers? A 2022 study linking linguistic, archaeological, and genetic data finds that the Bantu migrated from the region of the Gulf of Guinea eastward around 4,400 years ago.[3] With this migration, the Bantu brought with them their agricultural know-how, which promoted a sedentary way of life.

The Bantu presence in the south is so massive that those who don't speak Bantu languages are grouped together under the cover term Khoisan. Their languages are categorized into three different language families, Kxa, Tuu, and Khoe-Kwadi, with most languages either endangered or dormant. Speakers of these languages use click consonants in a systematic way, a linguistic feature that is not found elsewhere in the world (note that speakers of nonclick languages use clicks sporadically; for example, speakers of English use one kind of click to express disapproval as in tsk-tsk). Unlike Bantu farmers, Khoisans are herders, hunter-gatherers, or have mixed modes of subsistence. A 2021 study by CNRS biological anthropologist and linguist Brigitte Pakendorf and Max Planck geneticist Mark Stoneking confirms the genetic diversity of Khoisan people, in addition to their linguistic and cultural diversity.[4]

The second-largest language family, Afro-Asiatic, includes six language groupings: Berber, Chadic, Cushitic, Egyptian, Omotic, and Semitic. Over 300 Afro-Asiatic languages are currently spoken by more than 350 million people across the world, spanning North, Central, and East Africa, the Middle East, the Caucasus, and Central Asia as well as Europe and the United States.[5]

Between the Atlantic-Congo language family in the south and Afro-Asiatic language family in the north, we find speakers of a variety of language families living in the Macro-Sudan area.

Overall, in Africa, the numbers are reassuring: about 1,300 languages are safe, including about 890 Atlantic-Congo and 160 Afro-Asiatic languages.[6]

At the other extreme of the endangerment scale, over 80 languages are no longer spoken (including ancient languages like Ancient Egyptian and Meroitic) or are dormant and awakening—a figure much lower than what is found on other continents.

Today, 50 languages are severely endangered, having fewer than 100 users and no longer being passed down to the new generations.

Moreover, 23 languages have fewer than 10 language keepers. Even though you might not recognize these names, you can read them one by one: Bom-Kim, Bure, Dama (Cameroon), Goundo, Kasanga, Kwanja, Ndai, Ngbinda-Mayeka, Njanga, Njerep, Nyang'i, Nǁng, Ongota, Principense, Sambe, Sere, Sheni-Ziriya, Tagbu, Tiefo-Nyafogo-Numudara, Tombidi, Xiri, Yangkam, and Zaramo.

The greatest number of endangered languages is found in countries that also had high language diversity to start with, like Nigeria and Cameroon. In addition, many language families spoken in Sudan are currently endangered, for reasons that we will discuss in chapter 3 (e.g., Dajuic, Heibanic, Kadugli-Krongo, Katla-Tima, Narrow Talodi, and Nubian).

## Eurasia

Humans moved out of Africa and reached the Middle East (by 100,000 years ago), Asia (by 70,000 years ago), and Europe (by 40,000 years ago), where they met and had offspring with other hominin populations, like the Neanderthals and Denisovans, who eventually disappeared for unknown reasons, but whose genes most humans still carry today.[7]

At present, Eurasia is home to roughly 25 percent of the world's languages, or 1,600 languages.

Two language families stand out in terms of the number of speakers, Indo-European and Sino-Tibetan, spoken by half the world's population.

The Indo-European language family alone comprises approximately 500 languages spoken by over 3.3 billion speakers. The origins of the Indo-European languages are a hotly debated topic. In 2022, an international team of researchers traced Indo-European languages to the Yamnaya steppe herders in present-day Ukraine, with Caucasus and Eastern hunter-gatherer ancestry. According to analysis of genetic material, their expansion across Eurasia began some 5,000 years ago, when newcomers fused with local populations (e.g., Anatolian, Balkan, and Levantine people). This migration led to the subsequent split into the different Indo-European language groups (e.g., Balto-Slavic, Celtic, Germanic, Indo-Iranian, and Italic).[8] An alternative hypothesis, however, proposes that the spread of Indo-European language speakers started in Anatolia (in present-day Türkiye) between 8,000 to 9,500 years ago.[9]

While many modern Indo-European languages are endangered to various degrees, all Celtic languages were endangered until recently. Language reclamation processes have turned the situation around for many of them. I was pleasantly surprised to discover that Breton (Brittany, France) now appears on the Glottolog map as safe. Cornish (Cornwall, United Kingdom), Irish Gaelic (Ireland), Scottish Gaelig (Scotland, United Kingdom), and Welsh (Wales, United Kingdom) are still endangered to various degrees despite significant progress. Manx, a Celtic language spoken on the Isle of Man located between the United Kingdom and Ireland, is currently awakening.

The other largest language family in Eurasia is Sino-Tibetan, with some 500 languages spoken by 1.2 billion people. A 2019 study by a team of CNRS and Max Planck linguists finds that Sino-Tibetan languages were spoken approximately 9,200 years ago among Chinese millet farmers.[10] The majority of Sino-Tibetan speakers today speak Chinese. The predominance of Chinese is due to a process of language shift from different Sino-Tibetan languages to Chinese following the expansion of the Shāng Kingdom some 3,600 years ago. Today, Sino-Tibetan languages are endangered to various degrees.

Next to the two large language families, Indo-European and Sino-Tibetan, other smaller, albeit important, language families are found in Eurasia.

The Dravidian language family, for example, with almost 80 languages, has over 200 million speakers residing in Afghanistan, India, Nepal, and Pakistan. In a 2018 linguistic study, a German and Indian team confirmed that the Dravidian language family is approximately 4,500 years old, in agreement with archaeological findings.[11] At present, most Dravidian languages are not endangered.

The Turkic language family comprises 40 languages spoken by over 200 million speakers spread across a vast territory that extends from the Balkans, eastern Europe, and Türkiye to China and Siberia. In a similarly vast area, spreading from eastern Europe to Asia, reside the speakers of 14 Mongolic-Khitan languages. A common ancestor of the Turkic languages, called Proto-Turkic, goes back to over 4,000 years ago.[12] More controversial is the Transeurasian hypothesis according to which Turkic languages are distantly related to Japonic, Koreanic, Mongolic, and Tungusic languages.[13] Today, Tungusic languages spoken in Russia and China are particularly endangered, as well as various Turkic (e.g., Salar and West Yugur) and Mongolic-Khitan languages (e.g., Kangjia and Mongghul) spoken in China.

Moreover, in Eurasia, there are over 25 million speakers of about 40 Uralic languages, like Estonian, Finnish, and Hungarian. According to researchers, speakers of Uralic languages resided in the Volga River in present-day Russia. Some 4,200 years ago, they spread to the north and across Siberia. Recent linguistic studies show that Uralic languages had no connection with Indo-European languages until 4,000 years ago, when the two populations of speakers came into contact.[14] The Uralic Saami languages spoken in Finland, Norway, and Sweden are endangered to varying degrees (e.g., Inari Saami, Lule Saami, North Saami, Pite Saami, South Saami, and Ume Saami). In Russia, Uralic languages are also endangered, like Komi, Tundra and Forest Nenets, Kildin Saami, Skolt Saami, and Ter Saami.

The Caucasus is another linguistically diverse area that hosts approximately 8 million speakers of 40 Indigenous languages that fall under 3 Indigenous language families: Nakh-Daghestanian and South Caucasian (also known as Kartvelian), with homelands in the south, and Abkhaz-Adyge, a language family whose homeland has not been identified. Nowadays, most of these languages are endangered, mainly under Russian influence. Note that languages from the Indo-European and Turkic language families have also been spoken in the region for centuries.

Finally, in western Europe, Basque is a language isolate, meaning that it has no known closely related languages. Following a successful reclamation movement, over a million people speak or understand Basque.

In addition to the language families mentioned above, languages belonging to smaller language families are endangered. In Siberia, Russian expansion led to the endangerment of Indigenous languages such as Chukchi, Evenki, Koryak, and Northern and Southern Yukaghir. In India, the Great Andamanese languages spoken in the Andaman Islands are endangered too.

In Eurasia, more than 550 languages are safe, including about 200 Indo-European and 120 Sino-Tibetan languages.[15]

Roughly 200 known languages are either dormant, extinct (according to Glottolog's terminology, like the Indo-European Thracian language), or have considerably changed throughout the centuries to the extent that linguists consider the past forms are not in use (e.g., Mycenaean Greek, Old Chinese, Old English, Old French, and Old Japanese).

Indeed, as a speaker of Modern Greek, I cannot understand ancient forms of Greek without training.

Today, in Eurasia, 100 languages are severely endangered, with less than 100 users.

An additional 60 languages have even fewer language users—a trend that many communities are working to reverse through reclamation programs: Akajeru, Amami O Shima Sign Language, A'ou, Arem, Ayizi, Baba Malay, Bahing, Baraamu, Barzani Jewish Neo-Aramaic, Bih, Chiangmai Sign Language, Chukwa, Dezfuli-Shushtari, Dumi, Estonian Swedish, Gelao Mulao, Ghandruk Sign Language, Halam, Hokkaido Ainu, Ili Turki, Karaim, Khamyang, Krymchak, Kusunda, Lawu, Ludian, Macanese, Malabar-Sri Lanka Portuguese, Manchu, Mok, Northern Yukaghir, Nung (Myanmar), Old Bangkok Sign Language, Olekha, Orok, Pite Saami, Purum, Red Gelao, Romano-Greek, Ruga, Samatao, Samatu, Schiermonnikoog Frisian, Skolt Saami, Somray of Battambang-Somre of Siem Reap, Southern Yukaghir, Surgut Khanty, Syriem, Tai Long, Taiga Sayan Turkic, Terschelling Frisian, Tilung, Tosu, Tundra Enets, Udihe, Ugong, Ulch, Ume Saami, Vach-Vasjugan, and Votic.

## Australia

Australia was inhabited by early Australians and Papuans around 60,000 years ago.[16] During this glaciation period,

Australia, New Guinea, and Tasmania formed a single continent known as Sahul. The early inhabitants of Sahul arrived from Southeast Asia, which was connected to the Indonesian islands—a formation known as Sunda.

Over time, the original groups spread throughout Sahul, leading to linguistic and cultural diversification.[17] Prior to European colonization, Aboriginal and Torres Strait Islander Peoples used at least 440 different languages, and had distinct social systems, lifestyles, and cultural practices.[18] Multilingualism facilitated communication between the different groups, which maintained relations for marriage, cultural and religious reasons, trade, resource sharing, and managing the environment.

In 1770, James Cook claimed the continent for the British Crown, and in 1788, the British government launched a process of settlement colonization. European settlers brought new diseases that decimated the local populations and seized their ancestral lands by introducing the concept of *terra nullius*, a Latin term meaning "land belonging to no one" (a legal principle that was only overturned in 1992). We will discuss in more detail the planned and unplanned impacts of settler colonization on Indigenous peoples and their languages in chapter 3.

Today, researchers identify 358 languages in Australia, of which 227 are either dormant or in reclamation.[19] Two hundred and fifty languages belong to a single language family, Pama-Nyungan, but there are also some smaller language families and unique unrelated languages.

The language that is used by growing numbers of speakers is Kriol, a Creole language that combines an English lexicon with the grammar of numerous Australian languages. Kriol emerged when Aboriginal peoples speaking different languages came together after colonization. Kriol is the only language used by Aboriginal peoples that is currently safe.

In addition to Kriol, six languages are relatively safe: Alyawarr, Australian Aborigines Sign Language, Kukatja, Mawng, Pitjantjatjara, and Torres Strait-Lockhart River Creole.

In contrast, 41 languages are severely endangered, having fewer then 100 users.

At present, 45 languages have few speakers and are critically endangered, but this is changing thanks to vibrant reclamation programs. Let's list their names as a way of acknowledging their language keepers: Alawa, Ami, Amurdak, Bardi, Bunaba, Dayi, Dhalandji, Dyaabugay, Guragone (or Gurr-goni), Jawoyn, Karadjeri, Kayardild, Kokata, Kunjen, Kurrama, Lake Carnegie Western Desert, Lamalama, Laragia, Lardil, Mangarrayi, Maranunggu, Maridjabin, Maringarr, Marithiel, Mariyedi, Marra, Marriammu, Miriwung, Mudburra, Mullukmulluk, Ngalkbun, Ngandi, Ngarinyin, Nhanda, Nyamal, Paakantyi, Umpila,

Wakawaka, Wambayan, Wangganguru, Wiradhuri, Yangathimri, Yankunytjatjara, Yinhawangka, and Yuwaalaraay-Gamilaraay.

## Oceania

Oceania is a vast area including Indonesia, Melanesia, Micronesia, and Polynesia:

• Indonesia is an archipelago located between the Pacific and Indian Oceans, and is made up of a multitude of islands.

• Melanesia starts from New Guinea (the western half is part of Indonesia, and the eastern half is independent Papua New Guinea), and comprises Fiji, New Caledonia, the Solomon Islands, and Vanuatu as well as many other islands.

• Micronesia is an area in the western Pacific Ocean comprising thousands of small islands.

• Polynesia comprises thousands of islands, and includes Aotearoa New Zealand, Hawai'i, Samoa, and Tahiti, among others.

Oceania is home to the Indigenous Papuan and Austronesian people.

The ancestors of the Papuans reached the Sahul continent about 60,000 years ago, and their presence has been continuous ever since (you can read the section on Australia for more information about this early migration).

Austronesians arrived much later; one linguistic study traces their origins to Taiwan, 5,230 years ago.[20] Two thousand years later, the Austronesians reached Melanesia, where local populations were settled from earlier migrations, and then sailed into Polynesia some 1,200 years later. Then in the fourteenth century, the ancestors of the Māori reached Aotearoa and Te Waipounamu (New Zealand) in their double-hulled canoes.

The various regions in Oceania have different European colonial histories that are difficult to summarize. For example, Britain annexed New Zealand (in 1840), but the main European colonial power in Indonesia was the Netherlands for several centuries, while Chile, France, Germany, and the United States, among others, claimed other regions. Decolonization processes are ongoing. In New Caledonia, France, for instance, the Nouméa Accord signed in 1989 started a twenty-year-long transition process toward greater political independence for the Indigenous Peoples of New Caledonia, the Kanaks.

Oceania hosts almost one-third of the world's languages, or over 2,000 languages. Papua New Guinea alone is a hotbed of language diversity with some 800 languages spoken there out of the 7,000 languages in the world.

In Oceania, over 800 languages are safe, including 500 Austronesian and 160 Nuclear Trans New Guinean languages.[21] Overall, the colonial processes in Melanesia allowed for better preservation of the Indigenous languages than in Polynesia and Micronesia. For example, traditional multilingualism was maintained in Papua New Guinea despite the pressures of colonialism. Similarly, in Vanuatu, even though language communities may be small, transmission to children is generally robust.

At the other end of the endangerment scale, 61 known languages are extinct (in Glottolog's terms), dormant, or awakening.

Today, 129 languages are severely endangered, with fewer than 100 users each and little to no transmission to the younger generations.

Fifty-three languages currently have fewer than 10 language users—a number that is changing thanks to ongoing community reclamation initiatives: Abaga, Abom, Alabat Island Agta, Amahai, Araki, Arta, As, Ata, Bacanese Malay, Bangka, Bwenelang, Gorovu, Hawai'i Sign Language, Hermit, Isarog Agta, Isinai, Isyarat Lama Cicendo, Kamasa, Kanakanavu, Kavalan, Klamu, Kulsab, Lemerig, Lovono, Mafea, Maku'a, Mand, Mangaia-Old Rapa, Maragus, Minidien, Mt. Iraya Agta, Naman, Nasarian, Navwien, Nedebang, Nguluwan, Nigilu, Nitita, Panim, Pazeh-Kahabu, Petjo, Saaroa, Seediq, Suabo, Taje, Tanda, Tanema, Turumsa,

Unubahe, Ura (Vanuatu), Vivti, Wagu, Womo-Sumararu, Woria, and Zazao.

## North America and Mesoamerica

Humans peopled the Americas more than 20,000 years ago by crossing the Bering Land Bridge from Siberia to Alaska when the sea levels were low.[22]

The lives of the Indigenous Peoples of the Americas changed dramatically when Christopher Columbus, funded by the Spanish Crown, reached the Caribbean Islands in 1492. This marked the beginning of western European colonial rule over the entire continent, drawing on the Catholic Church's bulls that authorized Christian sovereignty over "discovered" lands that were not occupied by Christian populations (a legal principle that is widely known as the Doctrine of Discovery and was repudiated by the Vatican in 2023).[23]

In the early sixteenth century, Hernán Cortés brought present-day Mexico under Spanish rule, which was then expanded over the rest of Central America.

The history of the continent is further tainted by the violently forced labor of enslaved Africans during the transatlantic slave trade that started in the fifteenth century under the Portuguese and intensified in the eighteenth century under the British.

As we will see in chapter 3, the colonization of the Americas had devastating effects on the Indigenous populations and their languages.

At present, North America and Mesoamerica are home to approximately 500 languages. This language diversity predates European colonization and was significantly reduced because of it, with at least 182 known languages having become dormant.[24]

The greatest language diversity in North America is found near the west coast, indicating that most languages were first spoken there before their speakers branched out to different places.[25]

One such well-studied population movement is that of speakers of the Uto-Aztecan language family. A 2023 linguistic study shows that a Uto-Aztecan common ancestor dates back to approximately 4,100 years ago in what is now Southern California.[26] Speakers of Uto-Aztecan languages then spread over most of the Great Basin and beyond in the modern-day United States, all the way to Mexico and Costa Rica, with the Uto-Aztecan language Nahuatl being the language of the Aztec Empire.

Overall, just 71 Indigenous languages used in North America and Mesoamerica are considered safe, whereas 440 languages are endangered to various degrees.[27]

Among the most vital languages in North America is Navajo or Diné, an Athabaskan language. Languages belonging to various families such as Cherokee, Eastern and Western Canadian Inuktitut, Moose Cree, Northern East Cree, Northwestern Ojibwa, Severn Ojibwa or Anishininiimowin, Southern East Cree, Swampy Cree, and Woods Cree are considered relatively safe, while the languages Central Ojibwa, Dakota, Eastern Ojibwa or Anishinaabemowin, Mohawk or Kanien'kéha, and Western Ojibwa are more vulnerable.

In Mesoamerica, 11 Uto-Aztecan Nahuatl languages are safe, 10 are relatively safe, and 5 are more vulnerable. Among the Mayan languages, 4 are safe (Chol, Tzeltal, Tzotzil, and Yucatec Maya), 14 are relatively safe (e.g., Kaqchikel, K'iche', and Mam), and 11 are more vulnerable. Otomanguean is a large language family comprising about 180 languages, of which 24 languages are safe (e.g., Nopala Chatino, Puebla and Northeastern Mazatec, and various Zapotec languages), 103 are relatively safe, and 44 are more vulnerable.

In contrast, according to current estimates, in North America and Mesoamerica, 45 languages have fewer than 100 users and are severely endangered.

Over 70 languages have fewer than 10 language users, although the numbers of relearners are increasing: Achumawi, Ahtena, Arikara, Bella Coola, Caddo, Cahuilla, Central Sierra Miwok, Coeur d'Alene, Columbia-Wenatchi, Comox, Ditidaht, Haisla, Han, Heiltsuk-Oowekyala, Hidatsa, Hupa-Chilula, Ixcatec, Karok, Kashaya, Kawaiisu, Kiliwa, Kiowa, Koyukon, Lillooet, Lower Tanana, Maritime

Sign Language, Michif, Mocho, Mohave, Mono (United States), Munsee, Nez Perce, Northeast Sahaptin, Northern Haida, Northern Paiute, Northern Straits Salish, Northern Yokuts, Northwest Sahaptin, Nuu-chah-nulth, Okanagan, Onondaga, Original Costa Rican Sign Language, Panamint, Patwin, Pawnee, Pipil, Plains Indian Sign Language, Potawatomi, Quechan, Rama, Sarsi, Sechelt, Sekani, Seneca, Southern Haida, Southern Pomo, Southern Sierra Miwok, Southern-Coastal Tsimshian, Squamish, Tabasco Nahuatl, Tabasco Zoque, Tahltan, Tanacross, Tenino, Texistepec Popoluca, Tlingit, Tule-Kaweah Yokuts, Tuscarora, Umatilla, Upper Kuskokwim, Upper Tanana, Western Abenaki, and Yuchi.

If you went carefully through this list, you may have noticed that two sign languages are cited: Original Costa Rican Sign Language and Plains Indian Sign Language. Melanie McKay-Cody, a Cherokee Deaf anthropologist at the University of Arizona, has extensively studied endangered Indigenous Sign Languages in North America.[28] By unveiling the connection between centuries-long rock art and signs used by signers of Plains Indian Sign Language, McKay-Cody concludes that sign languages in North America must have been in use for hundreds of years. She explains that there were different regional sign languages, including the currently critically endangered Great Basin Indian Sign Language (Ute), Northeast Indian Sign Language (Iroquois and Oneida), Northwest Indian

Sign Language (Inuit), Plains Indian Sign Language (Crow, Kiowa, and Northern Cheyenne), Southeast Indian Sign Language (which has no known signers anymore), Southwest Indian Sign Language (Apache, Hopi, Inuit, and Navajo), and West Coastal Indian Sign Language (Chumash).

You may have also noticed that the list of languages with fewer than 10 language keepers includes Ixcatec (or Xhwani), the language I helped document in the early 2010s. Among the language keepers, Pedro Salazar Gutiérrez, a long-term defender of the language, passed away in early 2023 at the age of ninety-five. The other language holders are Juliana Salazar Bautista, Cipriano Ramírez Guzmán, and Gregorio Hernández García, who not only collaborated to record and analyze the language but have also been active in transmitting the language at school. Rufina Robles, Patrocinia Salazar, and her daughter Rosalía Ramírez Salazar have extensively collaborated in the language documentation project too, while Ignacia Salazar Díaz, her daughter Juana Guzmán Salazar, and Jovito Álvarez Guzmán were active in earlier revitalization efforts.

## South America

South America has been home to Indigenous peoples for thousands of years. In the sixteenth century, the arrival of the Spaniards led to the fall of the Inca Empire in Peru and the annexation of most of South America, apart from the vast area that is now Brazil, where the Portuguese established their rule.

According to Glottolog tallies, South America hosts roughly 400 languages; as in North America, this figure was higher at the arrival of Europeans. South America is unique from a cross-linguistic perspective as it is home to 64 language isolates—that is, languages that do not belong to an identifiable larger linguistic group.[29] This is a sign of its language diversity.

The greatest diversity is found in the Amazon. At present, Brazil, with close to 200 endangered languages, is also home to more than 100 Indigenous groups currently living in the Amazonian Forest and avoiding contact with all outsiders following their early violent experiences with colonizers.[30]

How did this language diversity arise? A 2023 study finds that language diversity in South America (as illustrated by language isolates) was shaped across time by periods of isolation from speakers of other larger language groups and preservation of identity in periods of contact with speakers of other language groups.[31] Combined evidence from biogeography, cultural anthropology, population genetics, and linguistics helps shed light on the complex scenarios as these general patterns are not necessarily found in each group.

For example, speakers of the language isolate Puinave, in present-day Colombia, showcase the scenario of preservation of language and identity in periods of contact. The Puinave had been marrying people from other ethnolinguistic groups from the area and participated in large trade networks that required some amount of multilingualism. The Puinave language accordingly shows traces of contact with other languages.[32] Yet despite this contact, the Puinave preserved their group and language identity.

Scientists reconstruct a different scenario, with group contact but no language changes, for the speakers of Kamsá, a language isolate spoken by the Kamsá people, who live in the foothills of the Andes in present-day Colombia. While the Kamsá were in contact with the Ingas, who now speak Inga Quechua, their language shows little evidence of changes induced from contact with Quechuan languages. A possible explanation may be that the Inga people spoke a different language prior to the fifteenth century, when they started shifting to Quechuan languages.[33] Quechua, the language of the ancient Inca Empire, attracted many speakers of other Indigenous languages after colonization. As a result, Quechuan languages are currently spoken by 10 million people in Peru, Bolivia, Ecuador, Chile, Argentina, and Colombia.

But a third scenario, showcasing group isolation, characterizes the Tikuna, who inhabit the area that is currently part of northeastern Peru, southern Colombia, and northwestern Brazil. Genetic studies suggest that the Tikuna people have been isolated in recent times, but were in contact in ancient times with several neighboring groups such as the Cocama, Murui, Uitoko, and Yagua, among others.[34] This aligns with the observation that the Tikuna language (another language isolate) shows minimal evidence of language contact.

Today, the traditional language diversity of South America is considerably diminished. Of the 588 known languages, 200 languages stopped being used long ago or are dormant and awakening.[35]

At present, only 32 languages are considered safe. In addition to eight different Quechua languages, Paraguayan Guaraní is another vital Indigenous language used by both Indigenous and non-Indigenous people, as is Southern Aymara, an Indigenous language spoken in Peru, Bolivia, and Chile. Creole languages, like Guianese Creole French, Papiamento, and Saramaccan, are safe as well as 5 national sign languages.

In contrast, 30 languages are severely endangered as they have fewer than 100 users and intergenerational transmission has been interrupted.

In addition, over 50 languages currently have fewer than 10 language keepers—a situation that can change thanks to reclamation initiatives: Akuntsu, Arabela, Aruá (Rondonia State), Arutani, Baré, Baure, Cafundo, Carijona,

Cauqui of Cachuy, Cocama-Cocamilla, Guató, Huachipaeri, Iñapari, Iquito, Isconahua, Itonama, Jebero, Júma, Kanoê, Kuyubi, Maijiki, Mapidian-Mawayana, Mapoyo, Mekens, Migueleño Chiquitano, Ocaina, Omagua, Oro Win, Pacahuara, Paraujano, Paunaka, Pisamira, Puruborá, Qawasqar, Resígaro, Reyesano, Sabanê, Sáliba, Shanenawa, Sirionó, Tariana, Taruma, Taushiro, Tinigua, Trumai, Urubú-Kaapor Sign Language, Warázu, Wayoró, Yabarana, Yauyos Quechua, Yawalapití, and Záparo.

## Key Takeaways

• In Africa, over 1,300 languages are safe. Of the 2,200 known languages, 86 are extinct, dormant, or awakening. Today, nearly 20 languages are critically endangered, having fewer than 10 language keepers, and about 50 more are severely endangered, having fewer than 100 language keepers.

• In Eurasia, over 550 languages are safe. Of the 1,600 known languages, 200 are extinct, dormant, or awakening. Today, 60 languages are critically endangered, and almost 100 more are severely endangered.

• In Australia, a single language, Kriol, is safe. Of the 358 known languages, over 220 are extinct, dormant, or awakening. At present, 45 languages are critically endangered, and 41 more are severely endangered.

• In Oceania, over 800 languages are safe. Of the 2,119 known languages, 61 are extinct, dormant, or awakening. Today, 53 languages are critically endangered, and 129 are severely endangered.

• In North America, just 71 languages are safe. Of the 693 known languages, 182 are extinct, dormant, or awakening. Today, over 70 languages are critically endangered, and 45 more are severely endangered.

• In South America, just 32 languages are safe. Of the 588 known languages, about 200 languages are extinct, dormant, or awakening. Today, over 50 languages are critically endangered, and 30 languages are severely endangered.

• As we will see in chapter 5, there are currently numerous active language reclamation programs across all continents.

# WHEN IS A LANGUAGE NO LONGER USED BY A COMMUNITY?

The generations of the children of Residential and Day School survivors have only English as a first language. To come out of that and learn our Indigenous language is complex and layered and healing and empowering.

—Jaskwaan Bedard, "Language of the Land," *SAD Mag*

## Debunking the Survival of the Fittest Account

When nonspecialists talk about language endangerment, they sometimes invoke the survival of the fittest account. Isn't it true that only the fittest languages will survive, and sad as it may be, it is simply in the natural course of things? The short answer is *no*.

Here's a quick reminder of your biology class. In 1859, naturalist Charles Darwin famously argued that biological species are subject to *natural selection*: generation after generation, the cumulative effect of differential reproduction by individuals best adjusted to their environment (thanks to certain inheritable traits) leads to the generalization of these properties in the entire population. A popular name for this process is the *survival of the fittest*.

You may now wonder, How do we go from the theory of evolution about plants and animals to thinking about languages? Darwin himself didn't resist drawing a parallel between the processes of formation and loss of languages and species: "The formation of different languages and of distinct species, and the proofs that both have been developed through a gradual process, are curiously parallel. . . . Dominant languages and dialects spread widely, and lead to the gradual extinction of other tongues. A language, like a species, when once extinct, never, as Sir C. Lyell remarks, reappears."[1]

The problem with drawing such a parallel between biological species and languages is that natural selection pertains to random variations, not the intentional choices of human agents, as in the case of language users. Another major difference is that languages are not transmitted genetically; they are the result of social processes. Hence Darwin's observations for plants and animals cannot apply to languages other than in a sketchy way. And as we will see in this book, Darwin is wrong in his observation that a language never "reappears": unlike species, a language can be used again by new speakers at any point in time (recall Modern Hebrew).

This leap from species to social phenomena like languages is part of a broader approach known as social Darwinism. Social Darwinism has its roots in Darwin's own writings and inspired the infamous scientific and social eugenics movement.[2] The eugenics movement minimizes the role of social context and instead seeks to rank groups of people in a hierarchy based on a biological index of fitness. Following the crimes of Nazi Germany, which co-opted the eugenics ideology, scientists have turned their backs on this movement, which is now discredited as pseudoscientific.

In 2021, the American Psychological Association apologized for promoting the ideas of early twentieth-century eugenics, followed in 2023 by a similar apology by the American Society of Human Genetics.[3] In its report, eugenics is summarized as follows: "Eugenic ideologies were embedded into American science, politics, and society in the first half of the 20th century. Eugenics exploited preexisting prejudices and promoted the idea that 'unfitness' was genetically determined. Extreme measures such as sterilization and genocide were utilized to restrict the proliferation of people deemed 'unfit.'"[4]

## Species Endangerment, Language Endangerment: Is There a Connection?

Today, it is common to draw attention to the parallel processes of language and species endangerment.[5] Like languages, it is striking to see that 41 percent of amphibians, 26 percent of mammals, and 13 percent of birds are threatened.[6]

In the 1990s, linguist Michael Krauss, founder of the Alaska Native Language Center, drew attention to language endangerment with these words: "Should we mourn the loss of Eyak and Ubykh any less than the loss of the panda or California condor?"[7]

But is there a connection between the two processes, beyond the fact that they are two pressing problems of our era?

For Marxist scholars, the origin of the present environmental crisis is to be found in the development of capitalism and colonialism, starting with mercantile accumulation from the 1400s to the 1800s and continuing with industrial accumulation from 1750 until 1980. This economic model aimed to extract cheap labor, food, energy, and raw materials.[8] As we will see in the following sections, the extraction of cheap labor, food, energy, and raw materials decimated Indigenous peoples, destroyed the natural environment, and led to the current climate breakdown. So in historical terms, the processes of language and species endangerment are connected as they derive from the same economic model.

Other researchers set out to understand more generally whether the natural environment in which humans live shapes their social organization and whether this in turn shapes language diversity. In one study, anthropologist Ruth Mace and biologist Mark Pagel report greater language diversity where there is also greater mammalian species diversity.[9] The connection between language and species diversity here lies in the assumption that when humans live in places where there is easy, quick access to food, they tend to live in smaller groups, slowly differentiating from other closely related linguistic groups. Overall, ecoregions that support more humans (higher population density) will tend to exhibit higher language diversity, and rich ecoregions (higher resource diversity) will likely lead to greater language diversity.

Recent studies suggest that of all environmental variables, the density of rivers along with landscape roughness best predict language and species diversity.[10] For example, the impact of rivers on language diversity depends on how navigable a river is. Rivers can be barriers to contact between different groups and drive language diversity. Alternatively, rivers that can be easily navigated will facilitate contact and sustain language homogeneity. In that sense, there are no universal or direct ecological factors that drive language diversity. Rather, environmental factors impact social organization and languages differently from one region to another.[11]

In fact, in many cases, social factors override environmental ones. For instance, small-scale societies in Southern New Guinea live in a geographic area without major environmental hurdles and maintain close relations between different language groups including through intermarriages.[12] But instead of choosing to use a single language, they promote multilingual practices (more about societal multilingualism in chapter 8). This explains the high language diversity that characterizes this geographic area. In contrast, political centralization through powerful empires and nation-states often leads to language homogeneity. In a nutshell, it is less about the natural environment than about language ideologies.

Let's now situate the current language endangerment crisis into its historical context, starting with life in modern nation-states.

### Life in Nation-States

Modern nation-states were first formed in Europe by merchants, professionals, farmers, and artisans who seized or effectively limited the power of the aristocracy and clergy.[13] Key historical events are the Treaty of Westphalia in 1648, Glorious Revolution in England in 1688, and French Revolution in 1789.

As the new European nation-states took control, they pursued and amplified ongoing colonial projects to the extent that sociologist Gurminder Bhambra argues nation-states were in fact imperial states, not just nation-states with empires.[14]

When colonies in the Americas gained their independence, throughout the eighteenth and nineteenth centuries, the model of nation-states was widely adopted. Similarly, as colonies in Asia, the Middle East, the Pacific, Africa, and the Caribbean conquered their independence in the twentieth century, they also opted for the nation-state model. As a result, the United Nations grew from the 51 member states in 1945 to the current 193 states.

Some nation-states appeal to multicultural values and effectively respect the language of the ethnic groups that compose them. Let's pause here to ask, What is the difference between an *ethnicity* and *nation*? In the *Oxford Research Encyclopedia of International Studies*, ethnicity is defined as the "shared cultural practices, perspectives, and distinctions that set apart one group of people from another."[15] When an ethnic group seeks to establish an independent political unit, we start referring to it as a nation.

In Europe, Switzerland successfully illustrates how different linguistic groups (French, German, and Italian) can persist under the same state structure in the form of a federation.

Yugoslavia was another case of a proud, ethnically diverse state. I use the past tense because during the wars of the 1990s, the rise of nationalisms led to the formation of a multitude of independent nation-states (like Slovenia, Serbia, Croatia, Bosnia-Herzegovina, Montenegro, North Macedonia, and Kosovo, with the independent status of the latter still in dispute), each with its own set of minority languages.

Similarly, following the collapse of the Soviet Union, the Soviet republics gained their independence as nation-states. Within the new states, the former national languages became majority languages and Russian became a minority language (as in Latvia, Lithuania, Estonia, Azerbaijan, Armenia, Georgia, and Ukraine).[16]

Indeed, in most cases, modern nation-state building is based on monolingual ideologies: one nation, one people, one language. Within these national *imagined communities*, linguistic and cultural differences among some groups of people are targeted by policies and programs with the goal to assimilate these groups to the dominant national language and culture.[17]

France is the poster child of this monolingual mindset. After the French Revolution in 1789, learning and using Parisian French was promoted to allow all French citizens to fully participate in democratic life: "French shall be taught in every commune where the local people do not speak French."[18] As you may notice, this law says nothing about not using languages other than French. The surrounding discourse was particularly hostile, however.

In 1794, Bertrand Barère de Vieuzac, the spokesperson for the Committee of Public Safety to the Convention, expresses himself in the following way (brace yourself for some insulting language): "Federalism and superstition speak Breton; emigration and hate of the Republic speak German; the counter-revolution speaks Italian and fanaticism speaks Basque. Let us smash these faulty and harmful instruments. It is better to instruct than to translate; it is not up to us to maintain these barbarous jargons and crude dialects which can only be of further service to fanatics and counter-revolutionaries."[19]

Like in France, the boundaries of a nation and national language rarely, if ever, coincide with the borders of a state. Competing national projects therefore often arise within established nation-states. These are met with different degrees of violence and oppression depending on the place and time.

In western Europe, several nationalist movements are ongoing. In 1979, for example, Catalonia gained the status of an autonomous community in Spain following a century-long movement for autonomy centered on the Catalan language and culture. In 2006, a new law granted the status of nation to Catalonia, but in 2010 the Spanish Constitutional Court changed it into the status of nationality. This fueled a political crisis leading to the 2017 unilateral referendum on self-determination organized by the Catalan government. In 2019, the Spanish Supreme

Court found nine Catalan leaders guilty of sedition, although they've since been pardoned by the new Spanish government in a move toward reconciliation. History is still unfolding.

In the Middle East, the Kurds are a large ethnic minority group that resides in Iran, Iraq, Syria, and Türkiye. Kurds have a distinct culture and speak an Indo-European language, Kurdish. Kurdish is currently one of the official languages of the autonomous Kurdistan region in Iraq, while in the other states, Kurds continue to fight for different degrees of autonomy. In Türkiye, for example, the Kurdistan Workers' Party began an armed struggle in 1984, and in northern Syria, during the Syrian Civil War (2011–present), the Democratic Union Party declared regional autonomy for Rojava. Despite the significant contribution of the Kurds to the military defeat of the Islamic State of Iraq and Syria, to date, there has been no international recognition of an independent Kurdish state.

Let's now turn to discuss Indigenous languages in (post)colonial states in our next section.

**Life (and Death) under Colonial Rule**

We have seen that even though endangered languages are found in all parts of the world, their distribution differs.

As figure 2 shows, few endangered languages are found in Africa while most endangered languages are found in the Americas, Australia, and Aotearoa New Zealand. What accounts for this difference?

According to linguist Salikoko Mufwene of the University of Chicago, this reflects differences in the language ecologies between exploitation colonies, as was typically the case in Africa, and settler colonies, as in the Americas, Australia, and Aotearoa New Zealand.[20]

In exploitation colonies, western European nations exploited people's workforces and local resources, but didn't settle massively. This doesn't mean that the colonization process was not violent, as millions of African people were murdered and their social structures disrupted. For instance, between 1880 and 1920, Congo's population decreased from an estimated twenty to ten million people as Belgium's colonial rule pursued the extraction of rubber, ivory, diamonds, and uranium.

Mufwene explains that in exploitation colonies, use of the colonial languages was confined to specific contexts, creating hierarchies where the colonial languages were at the top, but also allowing breathing space for most local languages.

Africans further strengthened their languages as they gained independence from western European colonial rule starting in the 1950s. Nonetheless, as acclaimed Kenyan writer Ngũgĩ wa Thiong'o explains, it is a long process to fully reclaim African languages: "I believe that my writing in Gikuyu language, a Kenyan language, an African language, is part and parcel of the anti-imperialist struggles of Kenyan and African peoples."[21]

In settlement colonies, like the Americas, Australia, and Aotearoa New Zealand, the arrival of tens of millions of European settlers took a huge demographic toll on the Indigenous peoples. Although scholars initially estimated Indigenous populations at low levels, current accounts suggest that the continent now known as the Americas was home to around 100 million people, the continent known as Australia to 750,000 people, and Aotearoa and Te Waipounamu to 100,000 people.[22] It has also been established that Indigenous populations declined by up to 90 percent after the European colonization of the Americas and Australia, and by up to 50 percent after the colonization of Aotearoa and Te Waipounamu (New Zealand).[23] This population decline is due to a mix of imported diseases, violently forced labor, and the expropriation of traditional territories by the settlers.

Let me illustrate this dramatic population collapse with the story of the Ixcatecs. The Ixcatecs currently live in Santa María Ixcatlán, a small village in the state of Oaxaca, Mexico. The village today has around four hundred inhabitants, but at the time of the Spaniards' arrival, Ixcatlán was a thriving center with an estimated population of between ten and thirty thousand. The region, which had been under Aztec domination for fifty years, surrendered to Hernán Cortés and his army in 1520. Two soldiers from Cortés's campaigns, Rodrigo de Segura and García Vélez, received Ixcatlán as a reward in 1522. Less than sixty years later, a report by Velásquez de Lara for the Spanish Crown titled *Description of Ixcatlán* puts the local population at no more than twelve hundred Ixcatecs.[24] The reasons for this sharp drop are the same as elsewhere in the Americas: forced labor, in the case of the Ixcatecs in the mines, and a deadly pandemic, known as *huey cocoliztli* in Nahuatl, that started in 1545 and spread from Mexico to Peru.

Under colonization, the Ixcatecs were forced to pay taxes to the Spanish Crown. Spanish was therefore quickly established as the language of relations between the new territories and the administration of New Spain. At the same time, few Spanish speakers settled in Ixcatlán. In this context, the Xhwani (or Ixcatec) language continued to be used by the survivors and transmitted from generation to generation. It was only in the early twentieth century, when Spanish monolingual educational policies were put in place, that the few remaining Ixcatecs stopped using Xhwani with the younger generations and started using Spanish instead.

Read the next section to learn more about how access to formal education impacts language transmission across the world.

## Life with Formal Education

Access to quality formal education and lifelong learning is a basic human right. Yet formal education has been one of the tools that states have used to achieve cultural and linguistic assimilation.

The most violent expression of assimilation through schooling is seen in the Anglo colonial settings. In Australia, Canada, and the United States, truth and reconciliation reports have established that for nearly a century, the governments forcibly took away Indigenous children from their communities to missions and residential or boarding schools.[25] In these schools, Indigenous children did not have the right to use their ancestral languages, visits from families were discouraged, and all communication had to be in English.

In 2008, both Australian prime minister Kevin Rudd and Canadian prime minister Stephen Harper formally apologized for these government-sanctioned schools. In 2022, Pope Francis conducted a pilgrimage of penance in Canada to acknowledge the Catholic Church's responsibility for the abuses at Catholic-run Indigenous schools.[26]

Such violent assimilation policies are not restricted to the Anglo sphere. In the European Nordic states, for example, truth telling and reconciliation processes are examining the trauma caused by residential schools for the Saami people.[27] In 2017, some attention has also been paid to French Guyana's "homes," run by the Catholic Church with support from the French state.[28]

Even when populations were spared such extreme, violent policies of cultural and language assimilation, the devaluation of Indigenous and minoritized languages was institutionalized in day schools. Stories abound across minoritized and Indigenous language communities worldwide about how pupils were punished and disparaged when they used their community and home languages at school and beyond. Ngũgĩ recounts his experience:

> One of the most humiliating experiences was to be caught speaking Gikuyu in the vicinity of the school. The culprit was given corporal punishment—three to five strokes of the cane on bare buttocks—or was made to carry a metal plate around the neck with inscriptions such as I AM STUPID or, I AM A DONKEY. Sometimes the culprits were fined money they could hardly afford. And how did the teachers catch the culprits? A button was initially given to one pupil who was supposed to hand it over to whoever was caught speaking his mother tongue. Whoever had the button at the end of the day would sing who had given it to him and the ensuing process would bring out all the culprits of the day.[29]

In my grandparents' village, in Northern Greece, the older ones recall how they were forced to drink highly concentrated resin oil if they were caught speaking Nashta at school. Similarly, in France, pupils who were caught speaking Breton were given a symbolic object (called *cow*) and motivated to denounce other pupils who spoke Breton if they didn't want to be punished at the end of the day (punishments included writing hundreds of times "I will not speak Breton" or helping to clean the school).

These kinds of policies took place in the broader context of nation-state building, and were informed by social, political, and scientific ideologies that relied on racist and discriminatory group and language hierarchies as well as general stigmatization of bilingualism involving these languages (more about this in chapter 8).

For instance, in 1867 in Aotearoa New Zealand, during the debate around the Native Schools Act that aimed to reinforce the use of English, a member of Parliament expressed themselves in the following way: "We can never civilise the Māori through the medium of a language [te reo] that is imperfect as a medium of thought. If we attempt it, failure is inevitable; civilisation can only be carried out by a means of a perfect language [English]."[30]

To enforce the English-speaking policies, speaking te reo Māori at school was often accompanied by corporal punishment. In one study, conducted in the 1970s, half the interviewees said they had been physically punished for speaking their ancestral language at school.[31]

As formal schooling became generalized, many parents around the world chose to also use the language of school at home to help their children succeed in monolingual education systems. The word *choose* is a stretch; had quality bilingual education models been available to them, they may have decided differently. Anthropologist Gerald Roche builds on the work of political philosopher Nancy Fraser to explain the difference between free and coerced choice in language endangerment. Roche argues that the choice to shift to the socially dominant language is a coerced one that results from the unequal distribution of material resources.[32]

Even when bilingual formal education in an Indigenous or minoritized language is available, it is frequently devalued. In Mexico, for example, Indigenous cultures are center stage in the national narrative using the symbol of the Nahua people in the Mexican flag and officially recognizing 364 Indigenous languages and 68 linguistic groupings.[33] But Ayuujk linguist, translator, and essayist Yásnaya Elena Aguilar Gil recounts in her book how bilingual teachers in Mexico earn less, schools receive less funding, and bilingual teachers are sometimes assigned to teach at bilingual schools that do not teach their own Indigenous language.[34] It is as if a French-English teacher were assigned to teach at a German-English school! At the same time, Spanish-English bilingual schools in Mexico are highly valued. This underscores the fact that bilingualism per se is not at issue but rather the use of an Indigenous language is ultimately what is at stake.

As Roche notes, hierarchies between social groups and their languages underlie the coerced choice of language users to adopt the more highly valued language and abandon the devalued one.

Another illustration of the effects of language hierarchies in formal schooling comes from sign languages. Based on language ideologies that devalued sign languages and only acknowledged the value of spoken languages, the Second International Congress on Education of the Deaf, held in Milan in 1880, proposed to ban signing from formal education: "Given the incontestable superiority of speech over signs in restoring deaf-mutes to society and in giving them a more perfect knowledge of language, [the congress] declares that the oral method ought to be preferred to signs."[35] As a result, all sign instruction was ended almost everywhere in the world. Even though the imposition of spoken languages was slowly removed from education since the 1960s, it was only in 2010 that the Twenty-First International Congress on Education of the Deaf rejected the 1880 resolutions and acknowledged the harm they caused.

While the use of sign languages in formal education is rightly celebrated as a milestone, it has the side effect

As Roche notes, hierarchies between social groups and their languages underlie the coerced choice of language users to adopt the more highly valued language and abandon the devalued one.

of replacing Indigenous, rural, regional, and local sign languages by national and international sign languages. Ami Tsuji-Jones, a signer of Hawai'i Sign Language (HSL), recalls how teachers from the mainland would use American Sign Language (ASL) at school and discourage the use of HSL: "They were haole [white]. They saw our language and said: 'What is that? I don't understand your sign. That's wrong. No, no, no. Let me teach you ASL. No, no, no. You're signing that all wrong."[36] After having been used by several generations of signers on the Hawai'ian Islands, HSL is now one of many sign languages being replaced by ASL.

## Life (and Death) in War Time

*What Is the What* is a book that will have you in tears. It is the story of Valentino Achak Deng, one of the Lost Boys of the Sudanese Civil War of the 1980s, written by novelist Dave Eggers.[37] The novel recounts how Deng, then just a child growing up in a village in South Sudan, flees the militia that attacks his village, survives lions and hyenas, and reaches a refugee camp in Ethiopia and then Kenya. Deng spends several years in the refugee camps before being admitted to the United States. Deng's story demonstrates how forced displacement disrupts intergenerational language and cultural transmission as people fight for their life.

Although Deng's language is not endangered, the Sudanese Civil War is one of the main causes for the endangerment of other languages in Sudan. Researchers Ahmed A. Beriar and Hussein Abdo Rababah note the effects of the war on Nubiin, the language of the Nubian people of Sudan, in addition to broad assimilation to Arabic and climate change effects (like droughts and desertification).[38]

The situation described for Sudan is common to other African countries as the ethnic divisions of colonial times continue to breed wars and genocides within modern states.[39] From the Nigerian-Biafran War in the late 1960s, to the Tutsi genocide in Rwanda in the early 1990s, to the ongoing Cameroonian Civil War between the Anglophone separatists and Cameroonian state, wars have killed millions and displaced millions more from their ancestral lands.

The devastating effects of wars and genocides have equally scarred Europe in the twentieth century. Let's never forget the murder of millions of people, including six million European Jews, during the Holocaust (1933–1945) by Nazi Germany along with its allies and collaborators. Jewish people had been living in Europe for centuries and spoke different languages that are all now endangered.[40] Yiddish, a Judeo-German variety spoken in eastern Europe by some eleven million people in the early twentieth century, is now only spoken by Holocaust survivors, some Hasidic and Orthodox Jews, and new speakers reclaiming the language. Ladino or Judeo-Spanish is another diaspora variety that was widely spoken in the Ottoman space following the fifteenth century expulsion of Jewish people from Spain and Portugal. Ladino is spoken today by just a few thousand people. In the aftermath of the war, Jewish people in Israel reclaimed Hebrew, illustrating how language use can pause and then begin again.

## Life (and Death) in the Time of Pandemics

Historian Noble David Cook has examined primary written sources from the period of the European colonization of the Americas to determine the precise role new epidemic diseases played.[41] Cook finds that major epidemics would break out every thirty years and become endemic in different regions, with devastating effects among the Indigenous populations. The early causes of the outbreaks are still debated, but later causes include various types of flu, measles, smallpox, and tuberculosis. The memory of these epidemics is still fresh among Indigenous peoples in the Americas through oral history.

So when the COVID-19 pandemic broke in early 2020, Indigenous groups in the Brazilian Amazon rainforest were quick to react. They not only self-organized to protect their communities but also took legal action against the Brazilian Bolsonaro government, which was ultimately forced by the Supreme Court to offer appropriate protection.

As the UN special rapporteur on the rights of Indigenous peoples, José Francisco Cali Tzay declared in 2020,

> Now, more than ever, Governments worldwide should support indigenous peoples to implement their own plans to protect their communities and participate in the elaboration of nationwide initiatives to ensure these do not discriminate against them. States must ensure that indigenous peoples have access to information about COVID-19 in their languages and urgent special measures need to be taken to ensure availability and access to culturally appropriate medical services. It is a major challenge that public health facilities are often scarce in indigenous communities.[42]

In the 2020 webinar "Not Our Apocalypse," Māori scholar Linda Tuhiwai Smith reminds us that Indigenous health and cultural practices across the world foreground the community in a way that made it normal to protect Elders and the most vulnerable during the pandemic.[43] Smith reports how Māori communities put checkpoints in place to control who entered their communities, delivered food and care packages to those who needed them, and shared information online by centering the needs of the Māori people.

The pandemic impacted endangered languages in various ways. One significant way is through the loss of some of the older adult language keepers who were also the most vulnerable to the virus. In the small community of Aperoi, in Brazil, for example, Eliézer Puruborá, one of the most active Puruborá speakers in language documentation, passed away during the pandemic, as reported in a *National Geographic* article.[44]

Another way that the pandemic impacted endangered languages was through the transformation of language learning practices during the lockdowns. Two Indigenous scholars from North America share their experiences. Chickasaw learner Kari Chew explains how she adjusted her practice by meeting daily with her mother on Zoom. During their meetings, they relied on available online learning resources and video recordings to gain some immersive learning experience. We will see in more detail in chapter 7 how learning an endangered language can benefit from digital tools and practices. In comparison, Mohawk learner Kahtehrón:ni Iris Stacey turned to Indigenous methodologies, spending time with her family gardening, and exchanging knowledge about the land.[45] More about Indigenous methodologies in chapter 6.

## Life in the Time of Climate Change

We are living in an age where human activity has a massive impact on Earth's climate and its ecosystems. Current climate change was set into motion during the Industrial Revolution in the nineteenth century. Average global temperatures have since risen by 1.2°C. The Intergovernmental Panel on Climate Change couldn't be more clear: ongoing global warming is mainly due to human activities conducted in industrialized countries.[46]

Climate breakdown, however, is disproportionally impacting the lives of Indigenous populations that are also the least responsible for it. Today, even when First Nations and Indigenous peoples have gained sovereignty and land rights, they still need to reassert these rights as they fight for climate justice and against extractive industries. Throughout Africa, mining companies cause irreparable damage to Indigenous peoples' lands and lives. In the Amazon, massive forest fires caused by agribusiness and mining companies have displaced Indigenous communities. In Canada, tar sands pipelines run through hundreds of Indigenous nations lands, contaminating their water, land, and air as well as impacting wildlife. In Finland, the Saami lands are subjected to pressures from mining, tourism, and deforestation without the consent of the Saami people. First Nations and Indigenous activists worldwide fight back against multibillion-dollar companies, which typically enjoy the support of national governments.

Ongoing climate breakdown and the collapse of ecosystems is directly impacting community efforts to keep languages strong by disrupting lifeways. Overall, climate change results in the change of seasons, prolonged droughts leading to soil erosion and desertification, increased storm intensity, extreme hot and cold weather, and massive fires leading to deforestation. All of these changes are catastrophic for agricultural and nonagricultural Indigenous populations, who are forced to abandon their traditional subsistence strategies.

When people can no longer live off natural resources because of such extreme weather conditions, they are forced to relocate to nearby cities or distant countries. They then join the local economies and gradually converge toward the socially dominant languages through pressures we have already discussed in the previous sections.

**Key Takeaways**

• Languages do not disappear because they are not "fit" for the modern world but instead because some groups of people are coerced into no longer using their in-group language.

• The formation of modern nation-states created the conditions for language shift to the dominant languages through mass monolingual education.

- European colonization led to the death of millions of Indigenous people and disrupted intergenerational language transmission by the forced removal of children from their families and more generally by devaluing Indigenous languages.

- Language use and transmission to new generations are deeply disrupted in times of wars, pandemics, and climate change as people fight for their lives.

# WHY DOES IT MATTER IF A LANGUAGE IS NO LONGER USED?

Learning our language [Wôpanâak] gives us a basis for why we view the world the way we do.

—jessie little doe baird (also Fermino), "Inspired by a Dream," *Spectrum*

**Language Rights Are Human Rights!**

In Boots Riley's movie *Sorry to Bother You*, African American telemarketer Cassius Green adopts a "white voice" and suddenly enters a world of professional success. Riley's political satire successfully builds on the observation that although we all have an accent when we speak, some have accents perceived as conveying competence and trustworthiness, and others don't. This is a common form of linguistic discrimination.

Other forms of linguistic discrimination are about whether people even have the right to use their language at home, work, and school as well as in politics and the media. We saw in the previous chapter how this kind of linguistic discrimination was ubiquitous in colonial settings and still is within modern nation-states.

To counter linguistic discrimination, language rights were first included in the Universal Declaration of Human Rights adopted by the United Nations in 1948 in the aftermath of World War II. Even though these human rights were not legally binding, they set the tone for legislations across the world.

But many wondered, Is there really a universal human? Is an Indigenous woman in the Amazon effectively protected by the declaration? It soon became apparent that additional instruments were needed to protect all groups of people in accordance with their needs.

In 1982, for example, the Working Group on Indigenous Populations was established, aiming to also bring Indigenous perspectives to the forefront. After more than twenty years of negotiations, the General Assembly adopted the United Nations Declaration on the Rights of Indigenous Peoples in 2007, with a majority of 143 states in favor and 4 votes against by Australia, Canada, New Zealand, and the United States. These four states have since reversed their position and support the declaration.

The United Nations Declaration on the Rights of Indigenous Peoples offers the most comprehensive framework on the rights of Indigenous peoples across the world. Article 13(1) refers to language rights as follows: "Indigenous Peoples have the right to revitalize, use, develop, and transmit to future generations their histories, languages, oral traditions, philosophies, writing systems and literatures, and to designate and retain their own names for communities, places and persons."[1]

The general right to learn one's ancestral language was already protected in the 1966 International Covenant on Civil and Political Rights (Article 27) and later in the 1990 United Nations Convention on the Rights of the Child (Article 30): "In those States in which ethnic, religious or linguistic minorities or persons of indigenous origin exist, a child belonging to such a minority or who is indigenous shall not be denied the right, in community with other members of his or her group, to enjoy his or her own culture, to profess and practice his or her own religion, or to use his or her own language."[2]

A more radical approach to language rights was discussed during the preparatory works of the United Nations Genocide Convention aiming to make states accountable for *linguistic genocide* whenever official policies oppose the use of a language in daily interactions, education, and publications.[3] Ultimately, however, Article 3.1

on linguistic genocide was vetoed and didn't make it into the 1948 convention. Nonetheless, the term is still in use among Indigenous rights activists across the world.

Why do these conventions consider that language rights are essential human rights? Let's start by looking at the impact of language on health and well-being.

## The Impact of Language on Health and Well-Being

During the 1830s, approximately a hundred thousand Cherokee, Creek, Chickasaw, Choctaw, and Seminole people were forced from their lands in the southeast of the United States to the west of the Mississippi River. Over fifteen thousand people died during this journey, known as the Trail of Tears. In memory of the people who suffered and died along the way, the US Congress recognized the Trail of Tears as a National Historic Trail.

Research shows how by removing Indigenous people from their lands, like during the forced relocation of the 1830s in the United States, and disrupting health-protecting spiritual and cultural practices, European colonization has taken a huge toll on the health and well-being of Indigenous people. For example, prior to European colonization, people in the Americas lived long and healthy lives thanks to healthy diets, herbal medicine, surgery, dentistry, ritual bathing, and the widespread use of medicinal sweat baths.[4] At present, in contrast, Indigenous people throughout the world are exposed to colonial-induced harms that drive diabetes type II, cancers, cardiovascular diseases, and mental health conditions.

As Māori professor Papaarangi Reid from the University of Auckland notes, health outcomes among Indigenous people cannot be reduced to genetic differences or individual behavior. Along with other Indigenous scholars, Reid's work highlights the epigenetics of intergenerational colonial trauma.[5] This historical trauma is added to individual lifetime traumatic experiences.

Intergenerational trauma and ongoing abuse, for instance, jointly explain the high rates of suicide among young Indigenous people in Canada.[6] Similarly, in a context marked by a continuous experience of racial discrimination, Indigenous people who grew up in residential or boarding schools are more prone to drinking alcohol.[7]

Researchers further stress the social determinants of health. For example, Indigenous people often live in food deserts, where they only have access to food stores offering little and expensive healthy food. Policies promoting healthy eating that do not address this key issue are doomed to fail. To make matters worse, Indigenous people across the world live in environments contaminated by toxic waste and other pollutants, subsequently restricting traditional subsistence practices that could ensure direct access to healthy food.

In addition, research highlights multiple restrictions to health services for Indigenous people due to cost, accessibility, and discrimination. To take one example, overdiagnoses and misdiagnoses were historically higher for minoritized groups when compared to majority populations with identical clinical presentations, and such differences persist in medical practice today.

What actions have been undertaken to address these health disparities? Western medical interventions have failed to deliver as planned. Indigenous communities are now moving away from Western perspectives that mainly focus on illness and are instead adopting Indigenous perspectives that focus on health.

As one illustration, the National Aboriginal Community Controlled Health Organization defines health as follows: "*Aboriginal health* means not just the physical well-being of an individual but refers to the social, emotional, and cultural well-being of the whole Community in which each individual is able to achieve their full potential as a human being thereby bringing about the total well-being of their Community. It is a whole of life view and includes the cyclical concept of life-death-life."[8]

In such a holistic approach to health, learning one's Indigenous language is a key component of the healing process. A 2022 review study of all relevant publications finds that the active use or learning of an Indigenous language has overwhelmingly positive health benefits.[9]

For example, a study published in 2007 hinted at differences in suicide rates depending on whether the members of a community were able to converse in their Indigenous language.[10] This factor alone, finds the study, is a good predictor of suicide risk.

Reclaiming one's Indigenous culture is so empowering for Indigenous youths that they also do better at school.[11]

Cultural and language continuity further protects against diabetes.[12]

Similarly, a 2020 quantitative study based on the National Aboriginal and Torres Strait Islander Social Survey confirms that speaking an Indigenous language has positive effects on social, emotional, and cultural well-being. At the same time, the study shows that physical well-being is undermined by factors that are beyond Indigenous people's control, like access to health care services.[13]

Community-based practices are currently being undertaken, typically incorporating language, history, and hearing stories as part of the healing process. For instance, community and Indigenous researchers have elaborated a land-based health intervention called *Yappalli*, a Choctaw term meaning "to walk slowly and softly," to reduce chronic diseases.[14] In this intervention, Choctaw women go through a walk retracing part of the forced Trail of Tears migration of their ancestors. During this journey, the women not only reconnect with their ancestral trauma but also center on their ancestors' strength and love for future generations. Language is a central component of the process. Moving beyond mere translation of Choctaw into English, participants learn Choctaw words and concepts in relation to well-being and health practices.

To conclude, novel Indigenous approaches to public health typically associate endangered languages in a holistic approach that holds the promise of improving the health and well-being of Indigenous people worldwide.

## Language Loss as Loss of Knowledge

Genetic transmission runs directly from parents to their offspring. Cultural transmission, however, is a long and complex process that involves parents, peers, kin, and nonkin. For instance, the color and texture of your hair are genetically determined, but the way you style or color it is a behavior that is culturally acquired.

Contemporary anthropologists have been critical of essentializing understandings of the notion of culture. How people style their hair is bound to vary from one individual to another and change over time. Indian American anthropologist Arjun Appadurai therefore proposes a view of cultural spaces as fluid, heterogeneous, fragmented, and constantly negotiated.[15] In this perspective, we can think of culture as an elaborate dynamic puzzle, with its pieces expected to change over time.

But European colonization shattered the puzzle of Indigenous cultures and scattered the pieces. In the face of adversity, Indigenous peoples safeguarded the pieces for new generations to build back the puzzle.

Language is one piece of this puzzle, and as such it holds together other pieces like myths, legends, religion, body adornment practices, rules, daily routines, production tools, rules for social groupings, age grading, family, kinship systems, play, division of labor, exchange, cooperation, and reciprocity. Some of the pieces are more closely connected to language than others so that disruption in language transmission has a strong impact on other kinds of cultural transmission (see figure 3).

Let's look, for example, at kinship systems. Kinship relations structure many aspects of the life of Australian Aboriginal people. Lynette Riley, a Wiradjuri and Gamilaroi woman and founder of the Kinship online learning module at the University of Sydney, explains that the first thing that Aboriginal people who don't know one another do when they meet is to identify their relationship levels: "Where are you from, what's your Nation, what's your Clan, what's your Totem, who's your mob, who's your family, who's your mother, who's your grandmother?"[16] How does language come into play in this process?

Linguistic studies show that kinship terms linguistically encode some kinship relationships and not others. In many Australian languages, for instance, speakers

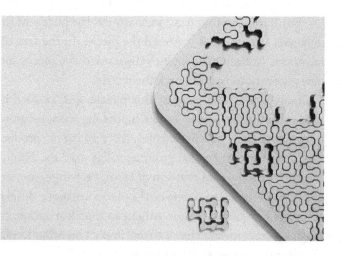

**Figure 3** Language and knowledge reclamation is like putting back together the pieces of a beautiful puzzle that has been undone. *Source*: photo by Clark van der Beken on Unsplash.

need to select a kin term to encode the relation between speaker, interlocutor, and the person being talked about. One should thus be able to use and understand a term that means the person who is my mother (relationship between me and the person being talked about) and your daughter (relationship between you and the person being talked about), with you being my maternal grandmother (relationship between you and me).[17] Using a language like English, where kin terms do not follow this Australian model, inevitably obscures the detailed insights that the kinship terminology of Australian languages offers.

Similarly, medicinal plant knowledge is impacted by language.[18] Think about it: plants are named by peoples who lived for centuries in a particular ecoregion and acquired rich knowledge about their natural environment. Settler languages, in contrast, developed in different ecoregions and lack a translation equivalent for new plants and the knowledge that comes from centuries of experience in managing the local ecosystem.

Paul Meighan, a Gael linguist from Glasgow, illustrates the strong connection between language, land, and water: "In Scotland, there are places in Gàidhlig that speak to the landscape and what can typically be found or encountered there: Alltan Èisg ('small burn/stream of fish'), Fèith Gaineimh Mhòr, ('the big sandy bog-stream'), or Loch nam Breac Mòra ('loch of the big trout'). There are even words that also speak to history and the Viking influence on Gàidhlig in my home islands, such as Clett na Cairidh ('rock of the weir' to denote a place to catch fish in Uibhist a Deas) from the Old Norse klettr ('a rock, a cliff')."[19]

Whenever Indigenous peoples were not removed from their land and land-related cultural transmission was not fully disrupted, knowledge and use of plants was passed on to younger generations independent from language shift. This is the case in the rural community of Santa María Ixcatlán, Mexico, where the Xhwani (Ixcatec) language has fewer than ten language holders. One ethnoecological study reveals that despite the loss of the Xhwani lexicon, the inhabitants of the community continue to use 627 of the 780 plant species inventoried by the researchers.[20]

This means that although culture and social organization are tightly connected to language, it is important not to conflate loss of language and loss of culture. This distinction is in fact essential for the younger generations that use a different language and yet strive to preserve the traditional material and intangible culture. Ixcatecs feel proud of their culture and aspire to preserve their way of life even though they no longer use Xhwani.

At present, Indigenous peoples throughout the world are reclaiming Indigenous ways of knowing and being through decolonization and Indigenous thought reclamation approaches. Nishnaabeg scholar, writer, and artist Leanne Betasamosake Simpson introduces us to *biskaabiyang*, a verb in Nishnaabemowin (Ojibwa) meaning "to look back," and in the context of thought reclamation, "returning to ourselves."[21]

In this cultural reclamation process, languages are an indispensable vehicle. Simpson notes that "learning through language" allows those who are invested in reclamation processes to gain rich insight into their culture by examining how the words capture specific cultural concepts and worldviews.

In a nutshell, while language shift doesn't equal loss of culture, as we have seen in the case of the Ixcatecs, language reawakening must entail cultural reawakening. That

In a nutshell, while language shift doesn't equal loss of culture, as we have seen in the case of the Ixcatecs, language reawakening must entail cultural reawakening.

is, language (re)learners should be able to (re)learn the history, knowledge, and practices transmitted over thousands of years. In practice, this means that in addition to learning the grammar of a language along with how to thank, greet, and accomplish daily communication tasks, (re)learners should be offered the possibility to combine this knowledge with cultural reclamation and appeal to culturally appropriate theories and methodologies.

## In Western Science: Understanding Human Language and the Mind

It's the year 3023. Following extreme global warming, there are no humans left alive. Aliens visiting the Earth decipher a paper published in *Nature* that mentions the *language gene* of humans. But there are no records left of any of the languages that have been used by humans. There is no trace of the thousands of spoken and signed languages used in different environments, in different times, and for different needs.

You get the idea: understanding human languages means going beyond what is common to all of us to explore the thousands of ways in which humans have adapted their universal capacities to different settings (before moving on, let me clarify that there is no language gene that we are aware of; genetics is more complex and cooler than that).

Languages differ in multiple ways that researchers haven't yet fully described nor understood. Grammars differ, sounds differ, words differ, and meanings differ. So when scientists aim to understand the universal human language and human mind, the narrow focus on English is detrimental.[22]

Notice I used the word *differ* to signal that there are no hierarchies between languages that are richer, better, more complex, or more modern than others. Researchers today explain that details of lexical categorizations depend on the cultural interests and communication needs of the people who use them. In the film *The Devil Wears Prada*, Meryl Streep's character is a fashion guru who demonstrates her impressive mastery of color vocabulary when her assistant can't tell the difference between two shades of blue-colored belts.

The same differences in vocabulary apply to differences between languages. Studies conducted among the Tsimane hunter-gatherers of the Bolivian Amazon show that industrialization increases the relevance of color with the introduction of a variety of colored objects. As a result, the number of color names in Tsimane increases. Stop and think: we rarely refer to the color of an object unless we want to differentiate it from another object, such as "I prefer the cerulean belt, not the lapis." For natural objects, the Tsimane meet their communicative needs without resorting to many color names since the color of natural objects is often predictable. Importantly, instead of color names the Tsimane can rely on an elaborate botanical vocabulary.[23]

Lexicon differences are straightforward. Let's now look at some more subtle differences between languages. In English, for example, we say, "The glass is to the left of the bottle," while we use cardinal terms to discuss larger entities, as in "San Francisco is north of Los Angeles." Yet one common way of describing small-scale arrangements in many languages in Australia and Mesoamerica is by using *geocentric* words and grammar based on cardinal points or other salient environmental cues such as mountains or rivers. Speakers of such geocentric languages would say something like "The glass is north of the bottle." If you take a moment to think about it, this is an extremely accurate way of describing a spatial relation because it is independent of the speaker's perspective.

This special attention to cardinal points gets trickier if your lifestyle doesn't involve a relation to the natural environment. Suppose you're in a conference room with no windows, in a city where you've just arrived. If you are using a geocentric language, you need to pay close attention to cardinal points before entering the room; your language requires that you pay attention to your environment in a way English doesn't. If, however, you have environmental cues available to you, you may rely on them independent of which language you use.[24]

Space relations are equally important to think and talk about time through metaphors. For example, in English, future events are in front of us; we say, "In the weeks ahead of us." In contrast, past events are behind us, as in "That's all behind us now." This back/front distribution of past and future results from our experience with bodily motion: we walk into the space in front of us and thus upcoming entities typically lie in that front space. It sounds perfectly logical, right? Maybe we could call this a universal? Not so fast!

Several studies reveal that these space-time mappings are culture and language specific. For instance, cognitive scientist Rafael Núñez and linguist Eve Sweetser found that in Aymara as spoken in Chile, the past is situated in front of speakers and the future behind them. This makes perfect sense: we know the past, so it is in front of us where we can see it, but we don't know what the future will bring, so it is behind us.[25]

In another study, cognitive scientist Lera Boroditsky and linguist Alice Gaby worked with speakers of Australian languages living in the Pormpuraaw community (Cape York Peninsula) and reported mental timelines following the direction of the sun.[26]

In yet another study, Núñez and colleagues noted that the Yupno, an Indigenous group living in the mountains in Papua New Guinea, gesture with the past downhill and the future uphill in line with topographic terms for spatial relations in their language.[27]

What seems universal to us, based on our experience with English, is quickly challenged when looking at other human groups and experiences. Focusing on widely spoken and studied languages like English is therefore biased in that it leaves out thousands of languages and ways to inhabit the world.[28]

In the past, the search for linguistic universals has been repeatedly challenged by novel empirical evidence. One such generalization has been that nouns are time stable. This is the conclusion philosopher Aristotle reached based on Greek, and that was repeated as an obvious and correct statement up until a few years ago. If you speak English, this makes sense since time is grammatically encoded in verbs: "I need the scissors" refers to something that coincides with the moment I utter these words, whereas "I needed the scissors" refers to a moment prior to the time of utterance. In contrast, English nouns do not grammatically encode time. English speakers can of course offer temporal information about nouns, such as *ex-husband*, *late grandmother*, and *former employee*. But all of this is temporal information we provide on a need-to-know basis using lexical processes, not grammar.

A more careful consideration of the languages of the world reveals the existence of languages that use grammar to also encode tense on nouns. I know this sounds impossible. If it *were* true, then speakers of such languages should be able to guess whether a noun is past or present based on nominal tense alone (no adverbs, verbs, or other contextual information to help). We tested this possibility experimentally with speakers of Pomak, a Slavic variety spoken in Greece where one definite article indicates past and another one indicates future (note that verbs have completely different tense markers). The task was simple: speakers listened to different nouns together with the past or future article, and then pressed a button on a laptop when they thought the object was in the past of the experimenter's life and another button when they thought it was likely to be in the future. In English, this is an impossible task: *the dress* is neither past nor future even though the dress a person wore last year at their cousin's wedding is different from the dress they are planning to buy for their friend's wedding. Results of this experimental task confirmed that Pomak speakers can indeed accurately categorize common nouns like *the dress* and *the friends* as either past or future without any additional information, and are slightly better when they know more about the speaker's life and whether they do have an *ex-boyfriend*.[29]

Another proposed universal that was abandoned is baby talk, the specific prosody that English caregivers use to talk to infants. Cross-cultural and cross-linguistic studies demonstrate that baby talk is in fact a cultural convention; it is, for instance, absent in K'iche' (or Quiché) Mayan.[30]

Other studies in language acquisition are attempting to quantify the amount and kind of verbal input needed for a child to learn to use language productively. Based on observations from middle-class English-speaking families, high amounts of verbal input and speech that was directed to children were celebrated as the golden standard. Yet recent studies from across the world reveal different patterns. For example, children growing up in subsistence farming households in Mexico, Papua New Guinea, and South Africa receive different amounts of child-directed and overheard language input. They learn to speak their languages just as well as English children do. It is therefore too soon to draw conclusions about what amounts and types of interactions are needed for baby humans based on our limited cultural and language studies.[31]

Yet another abandoned universal is the possible-word constraint concept, proposing that a single consonant or cluster of consonants should not suffice to form a word in any natural language. Although this may make intuitive sense for an English speaker, studies found that in Tashlhiyt Berber, an Afro-Asiatic language, some words are formed by mere clusters of consonants.[32]

In sum, languages differ in many ways. Still, languages have many things in common since they are after all *natural human languages*. An international group of researchers tried to look systematically at what was shared. The researchers coded 195 grammatical traits for 2,400 languages by using the information available in grammars.[33] For example, they coded simple yes and no answers to questions like "Are there definite articles?" (like in English, "the" banana) or "Is there grammatical marking of indirect evidence (hearsay, inference, etc.)?" (Turkish verbs express whether the information is firsthand or not).

Researchers then identified the most widespread grammatical traits and mapped their distribution in the languages of their data set. The statistical analysis shows that the language isolates (languages outside known language groupings) are more likely to use less frequent grammatical traits. Languages exhibiting the least widespread grammatical features are found in North Africa, Europe, and the Americas. In contrast, languages exhibiting the most widespread grammatical features are found in Asia. Rather than reinforcing the exoticization of some languages with "rare" features, the study shows that languages simply resemble one another when they belong to the same language grouping and have been spoken in the same regions (as we will see in chapter 8, unrelated or distantly related languages that are used in a cultural area start resembling one another and form *linguistic areas*). There is no mystery, really.

To conclude, we must promote a greater representation of language diversity in science. We can do this by explicitly encouraging the submission of papers from underdescribed and endangered languages in conferences and making sure to follow through with the publication of this research in international journals. Individual researchers can support this by changing their practices so that even when they study English, they don't take it as a representative of all human languages. One way of doing this is by naming the language under study (yes, even English should be named) and carefully discussing its potential for generalization across other languages of the world.

**Key Takeaways**

• *Language rights are human rights* captures the fundamental right of people to use their ancestral language in any and all contexts they deem appropriate.

• Languages are important for health and well-being as they help preserve the cultural pride and practical knowledge that come from using them.

• While language shift doesn't equal loss of culture, language reawakening should entail cultural reawakening.

• From the perspective of Western science, failing to embrace language diversity means failing to understand how human languages are used and how they represent the world.

# HOW DO COMMUNITIES AND GOVERNMENTS SUPPORT ENDANGERED LANGUAGES?

I can now sing a snow increase ceremony song in my language [Ngarigu], I greet people in my language, I can introduce myself in my language. Last year, I couldn't do that. It doesn't take very long to get a language going again, but people need to be supported to do that.

—Jakelin Troy, quoted in "Every School in Australia Could Teach an Indigenous Language" by C. Benedict and Sophie Kesteven

## How Do Communities Reclaim Their Languages and Keep Them Strong?

This is the story of jessie little doe baird, a citizen of the Mashpee Wampanoag Nation in modern-day Massachusetts. You may not have heard her story, but you might know that the ancestors of the Wampanoag Nation were among the first people to meet the Mayflower in 1620. At the time, tens of thousands of Wampanoag people spoke their own language: the Wampanoag language. In the centuries that followed the arrival of the first European settlers and then the migrants from across the globe, the Wampanoag people stopped speaking their language to their children. This was the result of a lengthy process that has its roots in the violence of colonization and power imbalance it created for the Wampanoag people (see chapter 3 for more information about the way colonization impacted language use and transmission).

When jessie little doe baird was born in 1963, the Wampanoag language hadn't been spoken for several generations. Later, when she became a mother, she began having dreams in which her ancestors spoke to her in their language. Not being able to understand them gave jessie little doe baird the strength to do something that radically changed the course of history for the Wampanoag language.

In 1993, jessie little doe baird cofounded the Wôpanâak Language Reclamation Project with support from her people.[1] She teamed up with linguist Kenneth Hale of the Massachusetts Institute of Technology and studied documents that were written in Wampanoag since the seventeenth century. Based on these documents and by comparing Wôpanâak with other Algonquian languages that were still spoken, jessie little doe baird wrote a grammar of Wampanoag and earned her master's degree in linguistics.[2] She pursued her work by compiling a Wampanoag dictionary.

With the full support of the Wampanoag people, she decided to put this knowledge into practice and organized Wampanoag classes for people of all ages. In her own family, her daughter and several grandchildren grew up speaking Wampanoag as their first language, marking the return of Wampanoag as a thriving spoken language. The MacArthur Foundation recognized this extraordinary story of successful revitalization of a dormant language and awarded jessie little doe baird the prestigious fellowship commonly known as the Genius Grant.

What do we learn from the Wôpanâak project? The first ingredient is to integrate language into cultural and political resurgence: this is known as *language reclamation*.[3] The second ingredient is inspirational individuals who bring together small groups of people around language reclamation. The third ingredient is the firm belief that change is possible, and that the language is alive although hidden or sleeping.

In language reclamation, communities start with identifying their own goals. These can include economic development, improvement of community health and well-being, land acquisition, sovereignty, and access to formal schooling. Importantly, language reclamation bolsters a positive relationship between community members and their language by questioning the societal and colonial constructions that led to their marginalization. In doing so, it increases pride in community belonging, a much-needed step in the postcolonial contexts where legacies of oppression, racism, and discrimination are still present.

For example, when I worked with a Romani community in Greece that is currently shifting to Turkish (the minority language for Muslim communities in the region), the priorities went beyond language strengthening. Access to formal schooling in this Romani community is affected by the broader social exclusion and discrimination that Romani communities are confronted with both at the local and national level, despite the recommendations of the European Union to promote Roma equality, inclusion, and participation.[4] Community efforts therefore went into organizing transport to help children access schools in the city, assisting families in administrative matters (as illiteracy levels are high among people over forty), and aiding adults to join lifelong education programs.

One way in which language programs can contribute to the varied needs of a community is to build capacity. CNRS linguist Pius Wuchu Akumbu, for instance, proposes that research projects could allocate up to 20 percent of funds for target community development (like the requirement that a project dedicate up to 20 percent of its budget for the host institution's infrastructure).[5] This amount could be used for anything that the community deems important or urgent. For language revitalization projects, one possible investment would be supporting schools, as it has been shown that having access to formal schooling allows youths to stay in their community, which in turn favors the vitality of the community's language.

As some communities fight for access to mainstream formal schooling, many movements of language and cultural reclamation decided to work with culturally inherent methods.

To take one example, in North America, the Akwesasne Freedom School, founded in 1979, is run by the Mohawk Nation, which provides immersion into the Mohawk language and offers a culturally rooted curriculum from the kindergarten level to the sixth grade.[6]

Similarly, in South Africa, one of the Elders interviewed by linguist Leketi Makalela stresses the significance of reclaiming traditional community-based learning systems: "Teaching was group-based. We would start with the group so the initiates learn together while the model men and women taught together. This is why I can tell you that we had a different way from the one we see in our schools today. Our schools fail our children now, but then we did not fail anyone. You don't fail when you are taught by different people who use entertainment and in many different styles. It would mean the community is failing."[7]

As some communities fight for access to mainstream formal schooling, many movements of language and cultural reclamation decided to work with culturally inherent methods.

Let's now turn to look at revitalization actions across the world.

## Language Revitalization Actions around the World

The Global Survey of Revitalization Efforts finds that most revitalization actions only started at the turn of the twenty-first century.[8] The oldest language revitalization actions started fifty years ago or more for the Celtic languages Breton, Cornish, and Irish in Europe, Anishinaabemowin (Southwest Ojibwa) in North America, and the Aymaran language Jaqaru in South America.

In language revitalization, language activities generally target audiences of up to fifty people. These can be either community members or outsiders depending on how communities choose to control who gets access to this knowledge. Learning the language in mixed couples is one way in which community outsiders are involved in language revitalization. Another way is when people take an interest in the local language and wish to connect with the culture.

The Global Survey of Revitalization Efforts reports that most language revitalization efforts focus on language teaching. Many projects have successfully introduced an endangered language in formal education. This is a task that requires funds and organization to create a curriculum and pedagogical materials as well as train language teachers. As a start, language communities can put in place such projects on their own.

For instance, when I was working on the documentation of Xhwani (Ixcatec) in Mexico, I witnessed the community's efforts to resume Xhwani classes in the community's schools. Weekly Xhwani language classes were set up in kindergarten, primary school, and middle school thanks to the collaboration of Xhwani speakers and local teachers. The Xhwani speakers, however, were the keepers of the language but had no experience in formal language teaching. Recall that Xhwani only has a handful of speakers left, most of them in their late seventies at the time of the language documentation project, and most having attended primary school in Spanish only, in keeping with the assimilationist agenda of the time. In addition, local schoolteachers teach in Spanish, and although some had training in another Indigenous language, it was not in Xhwani. So the Spanish-speaking teachers had experience with formal teaching but none with the Xhwani language.

Let me give you an illustration of how this worked. The teacher in kindergarten organized the class around a topic such as color names. They then asked the Xhwani speaker how one says "red" in Xhwani. The speaker pronounced the word: $ka^1tse^3$ (the numbers in the transcription indicate the lexical tones, which alone can differentiate the meaning of two different words; here [1] notes a rising and

$^3$ a falling tone). Then the teacher asked all of those who had some $ka^1tse^3$ color in their clothes to stand up and join them. They then asked the students to show the part of their clothing that had $ka^1tse^3$ color. This was fun as pupils actively participated in the class.

In primary and secondary schools, the class was more formal and included writing on the blackboard and focusing on topics that allowed pupils to work on Xhwani grammar explicitly. For example, the Xhwani speakers would list several animal names. Students then would notice that many animal names start with the same sounds. In linguistics, these are termed *noun classifiers*. The schoolteacher would then explain how classifiers for animals contrast with classifiers for humans, flowers, and objects.

Language teaching can take different forms, one being immersive language experience. The idea of immersive language settings is for every language user to choose an activity they like so that language learning reflects traditional language learning experiences.

In language nests, for instance, little ones can play, sing, and participate in different activities with older adult language users while their parents provide the physical work of caring. Language nests were pioneered in Aotearoa New Zealand, creating multigenerational spaces of naturalistic communications in te reo Māori with preschool children, and are now being used in many language communities across the world.[9]

These immersive interactions can be complementary with language teaching in institutional settings. For example, my daughter learned standard Breton during class at the Paris Breton school. Her school considered that exposure to other Breton varieties was also important and therefore organized immersive language sessions with an older adult speaker of dialectal Breton. As this person enjoyed needlework, they taught my daughter crochet while speaking Breton.

Immersive experiences are not only great for children but are amazing spaces for adult language learning too. To share one example, master-apprentice programs, pioneered by the Advocates for Indigenous California Language Survival, bring together adults with older adult language keepers in a deep family kind of relationship rather than in a classroom-type activity.[10] Teachers and learners explore several activities ranging from singing and dancing, to basket weaving and learning about nature. Immersive camps are another popular option that allows learning about the culture and language in an immersive way.

Moreover, partnerships between communities and universities across the world support language institutes that offer training to students, community members, educators, and scholars as well as researchers and language advocates. Let me cite here just a few institutes from North America that can serve as models: the American Indian Language Development Institute (University of Arizona, Tucson), Canadian Indigenous Languages and Literacy

Development Institute (University of Alberta), Institute for Collaborative Language Research (hosted at universities and colleges across the United States), and Northwest Indigenous Language Institute (University of Oregon).[11]

In addition to traditional and institutional spaces of language learning, innovative tech projects offer new opportunities to accompany the language (re)learning process. For example, twenty-two-year-old Danielle Boyer, an Ojibwa person from the Sault Sainte Marie Tribe in Michigan, has invented a shoulder-worn language revitalization robot, the SkoBot.[12] The SkoBot talks and sings in the Indigenous language in a way that associates technology with traditional knowledge. As many Indigenous people do not have access to the internet, Boyer made sure the robot runs without internet access.

Children and adult learners who do have internet access can follow language podcasts and visit online learning platforms. Anishinaabemdaa, for instance, is a language platform that uses flash cards to accompany learners of all ages as they learn the grammar and lexicon.[13] The digital format allows (re)learners to hear how words are pronounced and watch avatars pronounce them.

The digital domain of mass and social media is another space in which revitalization projects are deployed. If you think that endangered languages should be restricted to historical uses, ask yourself why this is not an expectation you have for English. The answer is not that English is more adapted to the modern world than languages that are being reclaimed. Users of any language can discuss any topic, whether by creating new words or adapting them from other languages. As Indigenous peoples argue, their languages not only encapsulate the knowledge of their ancestors but are solidly anchored in the modern world through the media, social networks, and internet too. As we will see in chapter 7, there is still room for improvement in this task.

Language revitalization initiatives also embrace all forms of artistic expression. From written literature and poetry, to the art of storytelling oratory performances, to cinema, theater, and TV, examples from around the world abound.[14] Verbal arts in Australian languages draw from cosmological foundations like "The Dreaming" and extend to children's games (e.g., nursery and counting rhymes) and various forms of speech play.[15] Music and song further illustrate the vitality of Indigenous languages, from the first opera in Noongar, an Aboriginal language spoken in Australia, to the popular Siberian folk pop band Otyken, which uses traditional instruments and sings in the Turkic languages Khakas and Chulym.[16]

## How Do Governments Support Endangered Languages?

Language reclamation starts within the communities. But today, modern nation-states have a role to play in language policy. A state has the power to recognize a language by law (de jure) in addition to whatever may have been the language policy in usage (de facto).[17]

For example, in Aotearoa New Zealand, English has been the de facto official language since European colonization, while te reo Māori and New Zealand Sign Language were only recognized as official languages (de jure) in 1987 and 2006, respectively.

Official recognition is not purely symbolic but instead expected to lead to practical measures that introduce the official languages into the legislative, executive, and judicial domains for which the state is responsible. Official languages can be further included in public education, health care, religion, and the professional world. These state provisions are part of *status planning*.[18]

Let's look at the language policy in postapartheid South Africa. Following Nelson Mandela's election as president in 1994, South Africa adopted one of the most progressive multilingual policies in Africa. The 1996 Constitution recognizes eleven official languages: isiNdebele, isiXhosa, isiZulu, and siSwati (referred to as the Nguni language group); Sepedi, Sesotho, and Setswana (referred to as the Sotho language group); and Afrikaans, English, Tshivenda, and Xitsonga.[19] Special recognition is given to the less spoken Khoi, Nama, and San languages, South African Sign Language(s), heritage languages spoken by immigrant groups like German, Greek, Gujarati, Hindi,

Portuguese, Tamil, Telugu, and Urdu, and languages that are used for religious purposes such as Arabic, Hebrew, and Sanskrit. In doing so, the state vows to take practical measures to support these languages in education, cultural and religious life, and the legal system.

Through such changes in status planning, governments attempt to reshuffle previously fuzzy and heterogeneous language practices by introducing boundaries and homogeneity. This is known as *corpus planning* and has been promoted by linguists in North America like Einar Haugen in the 1950s and 1960s as well as Joshua Fishman in the 1970s.[20] At this stage, the classic aim is to *codify* the languages—that is, develop a set of forms that will vary as little as possible among language users—or in other words, the goal is the development of a *standard language*. Such actions are typically carried out by language academies and special committees, even as they are increasingly conducted in collaboration with language communities.

For instance, in South Africa, the Pan South African Language Board oversees the introduction of official languages in the media, education, legal and administrative domains, and written literary production.[21] It also ensures the accessibility of speakers and signers to translation and interpretation in official settings. Moreover, the board oversees linguistic research, the development of technical terminology, and the reintroduction of place-names in the public sphere.

Though I cite place-names last in this list, reclamation of place-names is in fact an important provision in language policy. It was the first decree, for example, that the autonomous government of Catalonia signed: the use of Catalan in road signs, railway stations, bus stations, and public services.[22]

Sometimes it requires years of documentation to recover the traditional place-names. In Canada, the Inuit Heritage Trust received a mandate from the Nunavut Land Claims Agreement in 1993 to document the place-names in the Inuit language, Inuktitut, among the knowledge and language keepers.[23] At present, four hundred name changes have been added to official maps in Nunavut, and the process is ongoing.

Place-names are not only crucial symbols in decolonization processes that center the restitution of land but have additional practical value as they carry precious knowledge about the land and water. For example, Inuktitut place-names are records of the centuries-long experience of the Inuit people with the natural environment; the names convey information about the fishing lakes, walrus haul outs, locations for seal and caribou hunting, and areas with hazardous currents.[24]

A third major strand of measures in state-controlled language policy revolves around *language acquisition*.[25] Governments have a say when minoritized languages are introduced in formal education as they oversee the curriculum as well as train and pay teachers, at least in the public sector.

But language diversity resists official language policies and has been traditionally construed as a problem. Let's look at the People's Republic of China to fully grasp the challenge language diversity represents from an official language policy perspective. In China, Standard Mandarin is at the top of the language hierarchy, ensuring the communication of millions of people. In addition, 56 minorities have one officially recognized language. This, however, leaves aside some 150 linguistic groups that escape official recognition.[26]

In Tibet, for instance, Standard Mandarin is compulsory in education and employment. Standard Tibetan has an official status that is accompanied by several state provisions: a linguistic commission is developing a corpus, and Tibetan is used in the media and public signs, receives publishing support, and can be studied throughout school up until university. Yet many Tibetan varieties are ignored for the benefit of Standard Tibetan. Similarly, twenty-four non-Tibetic languages, including the Tibetan Sign Language, are not protected by the existing language policies.

In fact, for a language policy to be truly inclusive, governments would need to promote multilingual language policies that include all languages, not just national, large minority, and international languages.

This is what Nigerian education minister Adamu Adamu decided it was time to finally put in place. In 2022, he announced the National Language Policy, which allows any child to study in their first language during primary school. Hold on!—said some teachers. We have over five hundred languages in the country, and in some places, a handful of these languages are in use. How do we implement such an ambitious policy?[27]

India, a country with a strong multilingual tradition, has responded to this multilingual challenge by offering a *three-language formula*. In 2020, the National Education Policy confirmed this long-standing formula while introducing some flexibility.[28] Pupils can thus learn three languages provided that two of them are native to India. Nevertheless, the implementation of this policy has been confronted with the rise in demand for English as the medium of instruction.[29] In India, English is not just a colonial legacy but also the de facto language of a globalized economy. For many families, success speaks English.

To address such complex issues, institutional actors are increasingly consulting those who are impacted by language policies in order to align their agendas with the cultural, educational, and economic aspirations of language users. Language policy 3.0. is therefore a combination of what people do with languages, what they believe about languages, and how authorized bodies manage languages.[30] Authority, in this perspective, is no longer restricted to state actors but instead encompasses those who have authority over linguistic issues like families, schools, associations, and churches.

At the same time, family beliefs about language policies are shaped by dominant language ideologies. If you live in a state where standard languages are at the top of the social and economic hierarchies, then probably standardization sounds like the right path. If you live in a state where literacy is at the top of the hierarchy, then you probably think that your language's future requires being put into writing and the only legitimate way of writing is to go through a unified orthography. As linguistic anthropologist Monica Heller notes, most linguistic "struggles appropriate the principles of stratification in order to contest not the principles but the consequences of stratification for categories created by them."[31]

Let me illustrate this intricate relation between dominant ideologies and people's beliefs about language policy with Romani, an Indo-European language of the Indic language grouping. Romani is the language of the Roma people, the largest ethnic minority in Europe and one of the many European immigrant groups in the Americas since at least the nineteenth century. Romani is in reclamation in much of western and northern Europe, and is still in use in many countries of eastern Europe and the Americas. The most ambitious language policy concerning Romani goes back to the early Soviet Union (1920s–1930s) while more recent language policies are to be found within the European Union and in Colombia.

To understand how Roma envision language policy, we conducted a survey among Roma from Romania and

Colombia together with Colombian anthropologist Esteban Acuña Cabanzo and Romani Romanian linguist Cristian Padure.[32]

In 1995, Romania ratified the European Charter for Regional or Minority Languages, recognizing Romani as a minority language and offering the possibility to study Romani at school. In 2010, Colombia recognized Romani as a native language next to Indigenous and African Colombian Creole languages, but the language is not yet taught in schools.

The responses to our survey show that respondents in both countries strongly support bilingualism for children at home, believe that parental transmission of Romani is key, and that speaking Romani is primarily associated with interactions with family and friends rather than with formal settings involving outsiders.

At the same time, we found that while respondents from Colombia consider that Romani should be mainly spoken rather than written, respondents from Romania consider speaking, reading, and writing in Romani to be crucial.

Moreover, although respondents from Colombia declared that education could play a role in keeping Romani strong, they considered families and communities to be the primary agents. In contrast, respondents from Romania noted that in addition to the role performed by families and communities, education plays a central part in the revitalization of Romani.

Respondents from Colombia were also in favor of practical solutions that are less dependent on intervention from institutional actors. For example, they expressed their support for the use of Spanish words in Romani rather than the wholesale creation of new Romani words. In contrast, respondents from Romania favor the creation of Romani words based on Indic roots (since Romani is an Indic language)—a process that requires the intervention of a learned stakeholder.

The differences in the responses of the two Romani groups about the role of education show that once Romani is included in the education system, as is the case in Romania, it promotes a language ideology whereby language maintenance is ensured through formal education. Similarly, the use of Romani in schools endorses the significance of Romani in reading and writing as well as promotes top-down lexical creation processes versus everyday processes of lexical borrowing available to individual speakers. So what should be done?

Illustrating what a twenty-first-century language policy could look like, Aoetaora New Zealand combines official state goals with community-led goals. The current Māori language strategy, led by the Māori Language Commission, te Taura Whiri i te Reo Māori, acknowledges the need for a partnership between the Māori leadership and government of New Zealand.[33]

In this partnership, the Maihi Karauna takes a macro language policy approach that focuses on what the government can do and how it can impact the wider New

Zealand society. Here are the goals it has set to achieve by 2040:

- 85% of New Zealanders (or more) will value te reo Māori as a key part of national identity.

- 1 million New Zealanders (or more) will have the ability and confidence to talk about basic things in te reo Māori.

- 150,000 Māori aged 15 and over will use te reo Māori as much as English.[34]

Next to the government-oriented Maihi Karauna, the Maihi Māori was established so that a representative Māori body could lead its own revitalization projects. The goal of the Maihi Māori is to reclaim te reo Māori as the first language at home and in the community through immersion and community-led actions.

### How Do Intergovernmental Institutions Support Endangered Languages?

As states tackle the modern language policy era, intergovernmental institutions like the Council of Europe and United Nations raise awareness and provide guidance.

In 1992, the Council of Europe drafted the European Charter for Regional and Minority Languages to propose a set of measures in favor of minoritized and Indigenous languages.[35] The Council of Europe is also in charge of monitoring the application of the charter.

According to the European Charter's definition, regional or minority languages are those traditionally used by citizens who find themselves to be a numerical minority within a state. The charter's provisions do not apply to the dialects of the official language(s) or the languages of recent migrant groups. But they do apply to *nonterritorial languages*—that is, languages that were not traditionally used in a specific area of the state's territory (Romani, the language of the Roma people, sometimes falls under this description).

At a global level, the United Nations Permanent Forum on Indigenous Issues was established in 2000 and has since been promoting inclusive language policies.[36] For example, in 2003, the Permanent Forum recommended that governments should introduce Indigenous languages in public administration, at least at the local level in Indigenous territories. In 2005, it recommended that Indigenous languages should be included in the publications of the United Nations. It also recommended that states should support the inclusion of Indigenous language and cultural studies in universities. Furthermore, the UN General Assembly adopted the 2030 Agenda for Sustainable Development with the goal of ensuring equal access for Indigenous peoples to all levels of formal education and professional training. With this aim in mind, use of Indigenous languages has been strongly recommended.

In 2019, following the Permanent Forum's recommendations, the UN General Assembly proclaimed the International Year of Indigenous Languages. The International Decade of Indigenous Languages, which is led by UNESCO, began in 2022.

The major outputs of the International Decade of Indigenous Languages target access for Indigenous peoples to quality education in Indigenous languages; use of Indigenous languages and knowledge to maintain Indigenous food systems, biodiversity, and health; use of Indigenous languages to achieve gender equality, digital empowerment, and economic growth; use of Indigenous languages in justice; and finally, the establishment of a long-term global commitment to the preservation, revitalization, and promotion of Indigenous languages.[37]

## Key Takeaways

• Language communities across the world reclaim their languages in a holistic framework that involves community-led cultural and political resurgence; this is language reclamation.

- The first language revitalization programs started in the twentieth century, but the majority began in the twenty-first century.

- States and institutional actors have a role to play to achieve language justice by officially recognizing languages and ensuring their use in administrations as well as educational and legal systems.

- Postmodern and postnationalist approaches to language policy take into consideration how people act on and envisage language policy.

- Intergovernmental institutions raise awareness and provide guidance for inclusive language policies around the globe.

# WHEN LINGUISTS AND LANGUAGE PRACTITIONERS STUDY ENDANGERED LANGUAGES

For me, grammar is close to poetry. I think everyone hates grammar but it's wonderful, it's like looking at the x-rays of a language, seeing how they conjugate time and perspective.

—Yásnaya Elena Aguilar Gil, interview for *LeyendoLatAm* by Lauren Cocking

**From Research *on* Indigenous Peoples to Research *with* and *by* Them**

The returning boomerang is a weapon invented by Australia's First Nations. Shaped like a crescent moon with two blades of equal length, the returning boomerang swirls in the air and returns to the feet of the skilled thrower. A team of Aboriginal and non-Aboriginal education advisers, officers, and researchers who live in Wiradjuri Country invites us to think of Western research as located on one blade of the boomerang and Indigenous research on the other blade.[1] Researchers from these two ends would have to walk the exact same distance to the boomerang's apex to meet in a place neither Western nor Indigenous. This is the place where true partnerships among equals can be successful. But this has not been the place where most research on Indigenous peoples and their languages has been conducted.

Traditionally, research on languages used in (post) colonial settings is led by non-Indigenous religious missionaries and academics. In many cases, research was entrenched in colonial practices in which Indigenous participants and communities didn't decide what was researched, how it was researched, and how communities benefited from this research.[2] This research model is a kind of research *on* Indigenous peoples. It contrasts with research conducted *with* Indigenous peoples and research conducted *by* Indigenous peoples. Let's see what the two latter research models entail.

Research *with* Indigenous peoples refers to cases where researchers are conducting research in close collaboration with the community. In line with the community-based research framework, academic researchers must establish research agreements with the communities and appropriate community governing bodies. These research agreements must clarify project governance, goals, owner-ship, control, and dissemination of results. Community-based research projects typically seek to recruit citizen researchers from the community who actively participate in the elaboration of the study along with its implementation and approval. Appropriate credit and compensation are expected, including coauthorship in scientific papers. When applicable, it is preferable for the project to provide interpretation in the Indigenous language even when another language may also be used.

Most Western research institutions require that research protocols be approved by research ethics committees before implementation. Research involving vulnerable groups such as underrepresented groups and people who are economically disadvantaged are treated with caution. For example, it is prohibited to exercise pressure or allure potential low-income participants by exclusively offering financial incentives. The Statement of Ethics of the American Anthropological Association is a good starting point for a general reflection on ethical issues from a Western scientific perspective.[3]

Critics of this model state that in neoliberal academia, even well-intentioned researchers working in close collaboration with the community need to quickly produce scholarly publications that typically abstract away from the main goals and interests of the community. Therefore one form of epistemic injustice stems from the necessity to align with the research priorities of a predominantly Western academic audience in elite institutions where local contexts are of interest to the extent that they respond to a universal theoretical agenda.[4]

Participatory Action Research goes a step further than collaborative research and Western-oriented academic goals. In this framework, elaborated in the 1970s, academic and nonacademic researchers work together in communities to identify research goals that allow the community to attain specific political objectives. This means that the end goal of Participatory Action Research is to elaborate useful policies for the community. Language reclamation can be one of them. In Participatory Action Research, the concept of restitution of research materials to the community makes little sense because the research itself is conducted by community researchers in a process of *colabor*.[5]

At the same time, this split between community members and academic researchers is becoming obsolete since research is increasingly being conducted *by* Indigenous academics employed by either Western or Indigenous academic and research institutions. In doing so, Indigenous scholars are rethinking research ethics and methodologies in a powerful movement that strives to decolonize research and academia.

Linda Tuhiwai Smith of the University Te Whare Wānanga o Awanuiārangi in Aoetaroa New Zealand has been a leading figure in this movement.[6] Convinced that knowledge was an important part of precolonial Indigenous societies, Smith and other Indigenous scholars seek to identify what in their research comes from the Western perspective and reconnect with an Indigenous way of researching.

Margaret Kovach of the University of British Columbia in Canada, a scholar of Nêhiyaw and Saulteaux ancestry, notes than when conducting research with Indigenous peoples, many methods are Western; this includes the community-based participatory research and Participatory Action Research mentioned above. In turn, Indigenous methodologies offer a framework that is anchored in Indigenous epistemologies, theories, and ethics, and involves listening to stories and engaging with the community in a respectful and reciprocal relationship.[7]

In her book *Our Knowledge Is Not Primitive*, Cree and Métis scholar Wendy Makoons Geniusz explains that "the foundations of Biskaabiiyang approaches to research are derived from the principles of *anishnaabe-inaadiwiwin* (anishnaabe psychology and way of being). These principles are *gad-izhi-zhawendaagoziyang*: that which was given to us in a loving way (by the spirits). They have developed over generations and have resulted in a wealth of *aadizookaan* (traditional legends, ceremonies); *dibaajimowin* (teachings, ordinary stories, personal stories, histories) and *anishnaabe izhitwaawin* (anishnaabe culture, teachings, customs, history)."[8]

Indigenous methodologies are increasingly being used in research, and there is a will to translate them into terms that can be understood within the Western research tradition. One such methodology is *yarning*, a term used by Indigenous Peoples in Australia when they want to talk to someone. In the context of research, Indigenous researchers Dawn Bessarab and Bridget Ng'andu define yarning as an Indigenous cultural form of conversation.[9] According to Bessarab and Ng'andu, this research process involves four different kinds of yarning. It starts with informal conversation that allows building trust; the *social yarn*. The *research yarn* is a semistructured interview where the participants share their stories. The *collaborative yarn* is a discussion of the research yarn, allowing participants to share and explore ideas. The *therapeutic yarn* takes place after a participant has revealed a traumatic or intimate experience; the researcher then starts listening and offers support, though not in the form of counseling.

Even though institutional change is slow, Western institutions are increasingly acknowledging that Western science merely offers one perspective among many.[10] Indigenous researchers are seen as key actors to conduct research that pertains to Indigenous matters. In 2023, for example, the Australian Research Council funded the Centre of Excellence for Indigenous Futures, which relies on Indigenous ways of knowing and being to address inequity. It is entirely led by Indigenous researchers bringing together communities, government agencies, and practitioners.

But Indigenous knowledge is not restricted to Indigenous matters. Indigenous researchers are contributing to major global issues like the sustainability and management of the environment. For instance, in November 2022, the White House released a guidance report to assist US government agencies in incorporating Indigenous knowledge regarding climate adaptation and cultural burning into their research, policies, and decision-making.[11]

## In Search of the "Ideal Last Speaker"?

For a long time, and up until recently, linguists, anthropologists, and journalists would foreground the *last speaker(s)* of an endangered language. This approach is in line with the view that when the last speaker dies, the language dies too. Also, it helps a wider audience connect with the issue of language endangerment by centering on the lived experience of one individual.

No matter how well-intentioned the tributes to these language keepers are, they create a general understanding that it is the end of an era. By foregrounding the last speakers who learned the language in childhood, new speakers who may be (re)learning the language as adults are backgrounded. Indigenous and minoritized scholars have reacted to these limiting representations by inviting everyone to start projecting Indigenous and minoritized languages into the future.[12]

Linguists, along with language communities, are slowly learning to move beyond concepts of authenticity. Scientific perspectives inspired by the understanding of language as a complex adaptive system are also increasingly drawing attention to language uses by people of all ages and language experiences, whether they learned the language in childhood or later in life, or whether they are monolingual, bilingual, or multilingual.[13]

Let's see what such a shift in focus means in contexts of language endangerment. My former PhD student Eréndira Calderón conducted a study for her dissertation in a rural Indigenous community of Mexico where the Ngigua language is only known by a few people over the age of seventy, who currently use Spanish in their daily life.[14] As we have already seen in chapter 4, speakers of some Indigenous languages differ from those of Indo-European languages in the way they talk about space. Spanish speakers use terms like *right* and *left* and represent the objects around them in agreement with their own viewpoint (dubbed *egocentric*, meaning centered on oneself). In contrast, speakers of many Indigenous languages of Mexico refer to such relations using cardinal points and other fixed natural reference points like rivers and mountains (dubbed *geocentric*, meaning centered on the earth). This is different from *deixis*, where you point to the object you are describing. Geocentric descriptions imply that you have a map in your head and depict everything according to the map, as we show the location of countries on a map, with Canada being to the north of Mexico. In the same way, in geocentric languages, a glass is to the north of the dish, no matter where the speaker stands with respect to these two objects.

Given these two different ways of representing space, we asked how the bilingual speakers of Spanish and Ngigua manage with such competing representations of spatial relations. To answer this question, Calderón filmed the Ngiguas as they gave her a description of the location of several buildings in their community and a neighboring one (in order to exclude the use of gestures to point to the buildings). Participants in the study responded both in Spanish and Ngigua. Analysis of their verbal responses and cospeech gestures shows that the Ngigua bilinguals rely on geocentric representations of space in both languages and to a lesser extent the egocentric ones. The geocentric representations are most likely preserved among the Ngiguas because they continue to interact and pay attention to the natural world as they pursue their agricultural activities and practice small-scale cattle breeding.

Perhaps more surprisingly, the study demonstrates that the younger Spanish monolinguals who live in the same community also described the location of the buildings using geocentric cospeech gestures. Unlike the bilingual Ngigua-Spanish speakers, the monolinguals further used Spanish cardinal terms like *north* and *south*. They told us that they learned these terms at school, showcasing how formal education in the ex-colonial language, Spanish, can consolidate the local way of thinking about the world.

But how were the geocentric representations of the Ngiguas maintained when Ngigua expressions were no longer used and could therefore no longer support the geocentric conceptual representations? In our study, we propose that since the bilingual Ngiguas use cospeech gestures when they speak Spanish, these must have carried the geocentric representations over to the Spanish monolingual generations.

A few years ago, when I was studying Xhwani (Ixcatec), I also found that Ixcatecs who spoke Xhwani and Spanish as well as Ixcatecs who only spoke Spanish talked and memorized the position of small objects in space predominantly in a geocentric way and to a lesser extent an egocentric one. Some combined both options. For instance, let's say they were shown three objects in the following order, from left to right and north to south: a jaguar, rooster, and fish. When the speakers were rotated by ninety degrees, they could place the objects either in the same order with respect to themselves (from left to right, a jaguar, rooster, and fish) or keep the jaguar in the northernmost position and the fish in the southernmost position, resulting in a right-to-left order with respect to themselves: a fish, rooster, and jaguar.[15]

When I conducted a workshop with Ixcatec pupils in the primary school, they were fascinated to grasp their capacity to master different types of spatial memorization strategies. Being Ixcatec proved to be an asset, offering the possibility to recall objects as they were in an absolute way by relying on cues present in their natural environment (pupils felt this was the most accurate way too).

I believe that studies that include the entire community offer a new and much-needed perspective on language endangerment by highlighting the fact that sometimes local ways of thinking do not disappear. The feedback I got from the Ixcatec pupils unequivocally pointed to how this continuity strengthened their sense of pride and connection to their ancestral language.

The findings from these two Mexican communities are not unique. CNRS linguist Maïa Ponsonnet reports similar findings among speakers of Kriol (English-based Creole), who live in a community in northern Australian where the ancestral language, Dalabon (Gunwinyguan, non-Pama-Nyungan), is now known and used by few speakers.[16] The study shows that Kriol speakers make co-speech gestures around the abdomen region to talk about their emotions, like when they describe a feeling of relief, even though there are no specific abdomen metaphors in Kriol language for this feeling. Kriol speakers accompany these cospeech gestures with words such as *feels good* and *calm down*. In comparison, abdomen-related words to describe such emotions are attested in Dalabon and other neighboring Australian languages. Dalabon speakers use a word composed of *belly* and *flow*, meaning "feel good," accompanied or not by a gesture around the abdomen. This suggests that the Dalabon emotion metaphors have been transmitted to Kriol speakers through cospeech gestures by Dalabon-Kriol bilinguals.

In addition to embracing diverse language experiences when working in language communities where languages are endangered, linguists and language practitioners must also reflect on the significance of gender identities. Depending on their own gender identity, societal norms, and a community's leadership structure, researchers may find themselves paying more attention to men than to women or gender-nonbinary, Indigenous two-spirit, and queer people. But this offers just a limited perspective on the language community. As Hayley Marama Cavino of the University of Waikato observes in a paper titled "He Would Not Listen to a Woman," colonial versions of Māori stories excluded women as agents and knowledge holders while recasting men as protagonists.[17]

You may wonder, Why would gender matter in language description? First, gender often influences what people know, what they do, and how they talk about it. Up to today, gender specializations abound for housework

First, gender often influences what people know, what they do, and how they talk about it.

and caring activities as well as different professions. In the past too, human groups organized activities along gender distinctions (e.g., for metalworking, weaving, leatherworking, pottery making, house construction, boat making, and subsistence activities like hunting, gathering, fishing, and agriculture).

Gender differences not only impact the lexicon but can also sometimes change the grammar of the language depending on the speaker's gender; these are known as *genderlects*. For example, in Kukama (or Cocoma), a language spoken in the Peruvian Amazon by a thousand older adults, speakers use different pronouns depending on their own gender when they refer to a third person, regardless of this third person's gender.[18] For the Kukama speakers, the question "What are your pronouns?" might then mean, "What pronouns do you use (based on your gender) to talk about other people?"

Finally, the sociodemographic characteristics of language users are relevant. Western social classes are typically organized around occupational groups, income, and the degree of authority one has in the workplace. This results in distinctions between working-, middle-, and upper-class people or blue- and white-collar workers. Class distinctions are reflected in language use in various ways. For example, Queen Elizabeth II shifted from a conservative pronunciation toward a middle-class British English Received Pronunciation over a thirty-year period starting in the 1950s.[19]

Keep in mind, however, that Western-type social classes are intertwined with other social categorizations, like racialized and gender hierarchies, and, importantly, do not apply universally. Some societies have no social class hierarchies at all. Others have different or additional types of social hierarchies based on caste, clan, and religious or initiation status. Understanding the diversity of social hierarchies and investigating their linguistic component is therefore paramount.

## First Language Attrition

We often think that an endangered language will necessarily be marked by signs of attrition—that is, the loss of some elements of the language that were in use in a previous, presumably more authentic stage.

Thanks to the progress made in language attrition studies in recent years, we now understand that language attrition is a dynamic process that takes place at the level of the individual language user. *First language attrition* is observed when a healthy language user (understood as someone who is not suffering from Alzheimer's or has not suffered a stroke) has lower language proficiency than they previously had.[20]

Let me hurry to demystify first language attrition: its effects are to a large extent inevitable when people speak two languages, no matter how little they use them. Do you remember the last time you visited a country where they spoke another language and quickly learned to say "hello" and "thank you" in that language? You said it so often that when you came back home, for the first few days, the words that came to mind faster were no longer those of your first language but instead those you had been using in the past days during your visit abroad. You were experiencing the first signs of language attrition. This effect is limited in scope and time, and after a couple days your first language regains its habitual neuronal pathways in your mind.

Language attrition effects not only come fast but also go away fast. Research on immigrants returning to their country of origin shows that a language that has no longer been used can be reactivated after a short period of exposure. Additional evidence for reactivation of a first language no longer in use comes from cases of reversion of dominance among older adult migrants. This type of involuntary reversal confirms that the first language is still available in the mind.[21]

Sometimes, however, a traumatic experience can suppress the first language in a more persistent way; in this case, we refer to speakers as *silent* in that they understand the language, but do not or cannot use it in production.

Linguist Monica Schmid studied attrition effects in the German spoken by German Jews who emigrated to the

United States and United Kingdom under Nazi Germany. The researcher concludes that signs of attrition when using German are strongly related to the persecution experienced by each speaker: the greater the traumatic experience related to German, the greater the signs of attrition.[22] In Indigenous language reclamation contexts, cognitive behavioral therapy helps residential school survivors reclaim their first language.[23]

First language attrition is different from *incomplete acquisition*, a somewhat loaded term that aims to describe the acquisition process of children who weren't exposed to a language at levels comparable to those of other children. For example, studies show that if children are exposed to a given language only 10 percent of the time, then they acquire the language differently from children who are exposed to the language 100 percent of the time. These people are often described as *semispeakers*. Critics of this term argue that in the context of endangered languages, it can be perceived as delegitimizing and excluding (re)learners.[24]

Some researchers are aiming to identify the specific linguistic phenomena that are more vulnerable to first language attrition. It is assumed that linguistic phenomena acquired early in childhood and that are rules based, such as syntax and phonology, are immune to first language attrition. In contrast, the lexicon, which is acquired gradually throughout life, is more vulnerable. In line with this prediction, researchers note that the lexicon is particularly volatile: we forget words easily, but we better remember how to use their singular and plural forms.

Finally, aging impacts various language skills. We saw in the previous section how Queen Elizabeth II changed her pronunciation from a conservative to a middle-class one. But researchers noted that later in life, she resumed her 1950s' pronunciation. Their hypothesis to account for this trajectory is that younger adult speakers tend to converge with their interlocutors effortlessly and unconsciously; this effect is weaker in older adults for reasons related to healthy aging. As users of endangered languages are frequently older adults, it is therefore important not to conflate the mild cognitive effects of aging with first language attrition effects. If a language user struggles to remember a word, maybe it's just an effect of healthy aging, not a sign of general language attrition.


## Studying Endangered Languages

When studying an endangered language, linguists have traditionally pursued three goals: to write a grammar (or a grammatical sketch), compile a dictionary, and collect as many stories as possible; this is sometimes referred to as the "Boasian" tradition (from early twentieth-century German American anthropologist Franz Boas). As we will see, when adjusted, these goals can contribute to some extent to language reclamation efforts.

## Write a Grammar

Does every language have a grammar? Absolutely, every language has a grammar in every speaker's and signer's mind, shaped through the interactions this person has with other language users. Does every language have a grammar book? No. Only 60 percent of all languages have at least a sketch grammar.[25] The remaining 40 percent have at most writings in a few religious texts or a short word list.

Tackling a new unknown grammar is a highly complex task. Without training, we tend to start from what we know in our languages and project it onto the language that is being described. *Verbs mark tense, and nouns don't.* As we saw in chapter 4, this is not necessarily true. Training in linguistics therefore allows researchers to begin with an open mind to grasp the subtleties of the grammar under study.

To write a grammar, one can observe language uses, describe them, analyze them, classify them, measure them, and abstract away from them to better explain them, make predictions, and test these predictions. In a way, it is a never-ending task. Just think that there are hundreds of linguists working on English who haven't yet unraveled all of its secrets.

So how do you approach a language that has never been described? Researchers, whether speakers and signers of the language or not, can rely on a variety of methods.

For speakers and signers, introspection is one way to start. It allows them to know which structures can be used in the language and which cannot. But introspection only captures the way one person uses the language, not the way others use it. Do you speak like your teen nephew or your distant cousin who lives at the other end of the country? Chances are you don't.

Another classic method in linguistics is elicitation. This opens your research to a larger number of users to capture some of the language variation. In elicitation through translation, the linguist asks the language consultant direct questions like "How do you say, 'I offered a blue pen to the child?'" The language consultant translates this phrase into the target language. This method is straightforward, but it comes with some setbacks.

For example, we now know that a specific grammatical structure in one language can be carried over into another language through what is called *cross-language priming*. In one study, we find that when Romanian-Romani bilinguals read a sentence in Romanian where the adjective follows the noun (literally "pen blue"), they tend to use the same noun-adjective order in the immediately following Romani phrase (also saying "pen blue").[26] Otherwise, Romani speakers tend to use the adjective-noun order, as in "blue pen." This priming effect across two languages is more pronounced in elicitation through translation where the two languages are constantly activated in the bilingual's mind.

Moreover, elicitation through translation is a task that some language consultants enjoy and others hate. Sometimes these differences are due to differences in access to formal education and literacy. One classic elicitation task in linguistics is to ask a consultant to list the words beginning with the sound *b*, or find words that start with *b* and words that start with *p* and have different meaning (like *bill* and *pill* in English). *B* and *p* are dubbed *phonemes* as they alone can change the meaning of two words in English. But we now know that illiterate adults are uncomfortable with explicit phoneme manipulation, even though they are sensitive to meaningful differences in their language's sounds (i.e., they can hear that *bill* and *pill* are different, but will not think of them to illustrate the difference between *b* and *p* to a linguist).[27] Such elicitation tasks thus exclude some speakers needlessly.

More generally, speakers who have little formal education may not feel comfortable with school-type tasks like exploring grammatical paradigms. No language user will spontaneously offer the paradigm for the verb *to be* as in *I am*, *you are*, and so on. This only comes after formal training. Similarly, in elicitation through translation, a common first reaction for a consultant who is asked to translate a phrase like "I have two children" is to respond, "You have two children." This makes perfect sense since languages are typically used in interactional contexts where one user's *I* must become *you* during the exchange.

Instead of asking this kind of elicitation question to language consultants who may have had little formal schooling, linguists decided that it was a better idea to record naturalistic discourse produced in ecologically valid situations. This is also a much more pleasant and socially meaningful task as people get the opportunity to share their life stories, narrate tales, or have conversations with their friends and families about local history, life stories, and everyday life.

In practice, it's best to adapt to the wishes, habits, and possibilities of language production within a community. For example, during the language documentation program of Xhwani (Ixcatec), the types of collected texts depended on the speakers' preferences. Rufina Robles and Juliana Salazar Bautista preferred to record conversations about what was happening in their lives and the village. The resulting vivid conversations had frequent overlaps, back-channeling (like "uh-huh," "yeah," and "hmm"), and quick turn taking (an average of 220 milliseconds). Pedro Salazar Gutiérrez and Cipriano Ramírez Guzmán preferred recording conversations on the history and traditions of the community in a more pedagogical format. Turn taking was slower (an average of 1,000 milliseconds), with few overlaps and back-channels. Both kinds of language production are important.[28]

Some say that the naturalistic language production method also comes with its own set of problems. For example, when we talk spontaneously, we may use a word in the place of another or go a bit fast on its pronunciation. Sometimes speakers recover these kinds of production errors explicitly; I hear this on radio interviews all the time. At other times, speakers will listen to a recording of their speech and not believe it's them making these silly errors. Linguists therefore must keep in mind that disfluencies and errors in production are an integral part of language use and double check when needed. There's no need to panic over these errors, though; we generally make one error every thousand words.[29]

To complement spontaneous language productions, researchers often use pictures and films as elicitation stimuli. This kind of elicitation bypasses translation and allows linguists to systematically explore a specific topic and quickly compare the usage of many people. One idea is to use silent films like Charlie Chaplin classics and ask your language consultants to describe the film. Or you might want to produce your own color films and colorful pictures within the community. It's more work, but it's better to propose culturally adapted elicitation stimuli to participants of different ages and with different formal education experiences.[30]

The output of this linguistic analysis can be a grammar and scientific articles for specialists. Importantly, a pedagogical version of these findings is a vital tool for language learners in contexts of language reclamation. When possible, grammar authors provide links to the original audio and video files illustrating how specific language users apply the grammatical rules in language production.

**Compile a Dictionary**

Researchers often start working on a language by preparing lists of words and their translations in the shared, socially dominant language. When intensified, this work can create a full-fledged dictionary, with each word accompanied by a definition. As a researcher, I was extremely grateful to be able to rely on the dictionary that Xhwani speaker Doroteo Jiménez and Mexican linguist María Teresa Fernández de Miranda wrote in the 1950s. I was not alone. The Xhwani speakers who taught the language at school consulted the dictionary to help them organize their classes.

Indeed, language practitioners and language learners across the world value dictionaries. This is what motivated Lena Smith-Tutin and Vivian Smith, two residential school survivors and language teachers from Canada, to compile a dictionary of their ancestral language, Dän k'è or Southern Tutchone.[31] The result is a seventy-seven-page pocket-size dictionary that offers a translation for hundreds of essential words from English to Dän k'è that language (re)learners can carry around with them.

A digital format was chosen by the linguists and language communities for the dictionaries in the Australian languages Bilinarra, Gurindji, Mudburra, and Ngarinyma.[32] These e-dictionaries organize words along semantic fields and grammatical categories ranging from the environment, to food and cooking, to verbs and pronouns, and so on. Bilinarra, Gurindji, Mudburra, and Ngarinyma words are accompanied by an English translation and illustrations as well as audio files that allow interested users and language learners to listen to the pronunciation. In addition, plants, animals, and cultural practices are introduced along with encyclopedic information.

## Compile a Corpus of Stories

Following the Western philological tradition of the times, Boas was interested in Native American texts and verbal art, which he understood as a window into the language and culture of Indigenous peoples.[33]

Boas's influence is apparent in the studies of American languages throughout the twentieth century and up to today. Most texts were myths, folktales, and a few historical narratives. Early on, there were a few prayers, Indigenous and Christian, and later, humorous tales, narratives of lived experiences, songs, texts about how people lived and did things, laws, and conversations. This interest in all kinds of language production is maintained in current *language documentation* projects, aiming to record and preserve all possible language uses for future generations.

The texts that Boas analyzed were either transcribed from dictation by speakers of the languages under study or written directly by them. For instance, Boas collaborated with an Indigenous scholar, George Hunt, a speaker of Kwak'wala. Boas would sometimes anonymize Hunt's productions, however, in line with European folklore traditions, but by doing so removed Hunt's authorship. Moreover, in the folklore tradition, once stories were recorded and published in one way, they became fixed in time. Importantly, Western scholars would sometimes make changes, like romanticizing stories and removing sexual content or replacing female participants with male ones, and misinterpreting the stories' meaning through the lens of the outsider observer.[34] Today, Indigenous peoples reclaim their stories and retell them to transmit knowledge in a relational and dynamic way, in line with the way stories were told prior to European colonization.[35]

Stories and conversations also have particular significance in language reclamation. While grammars and dictionaries are useful tools in adult language learning, this is not how languages are traditionally learned and performed. To assist language learners and users, linguist Arok Wolvengrey, a series editor at the University of Regina Press, aims to publish language readers in all sixty-plus Indigenous languages of Canada.[36] As we will see in chapter 7, such stories and conversations are now increasingly available in digital formats that allow language (re)learners to listen and watch the language users in an immersive-like format.

**Key Takeaways**

• To study an endangered language, linguists are moving away from research on Indigenous and minoritized peoples to research with and by Indigenous and minoritized peoples.

• Linguists and communities honor and value the language keepers of endangered languages. At the same time, we must also acknowledge the value of new generations of language users as they reclaim their languages.

• Users of endangered languages sometimes forget their first language when they don't use it anymore or the language is associated with trauma. With practice and reexposure, the words and grammar are reactivated in the user's mind.

• The three classic outputs in the study of an endangered language are a grammar, dictionary, and corpus of stories.

# ENDANGERED LANGUAGES IN A DIGITAL WORLD

While we recognise the value of open-source, we also realise the majority of our people don't have the resources to take advantage of it.

—Peter-Lucas Jones, quoted in "Māori Are Trying to Save Their Language from Big Tech" by Donavyn Coffey

## How Does Language Shape Experience on the Internet?

I was just about to start college when the World Wide Web was launched in 1991. In the 1990s, during the first years of the internet, if one had an internet connection, they could visit a static website. But in the early 2000s, dynamic websites and blogs began to flourish and gave way to Web 2.0, along with streaming services like YouTube and Spotify as well as social media like Facebook and Twitter. This is how the internet rapidly came to structure the private and professional lives of billions of people across the globe. Today, 59 percent of the world's population has access to a mobile or fixed-line internet connection at home.[1]

The internet also changed the traditional news channels of communication by adding novel digital ones. The written press, radios, and TV networks have joined in the competition for stories going viral in global digital spaces.

At the same time, the internet enabled traditionally marginalized groups to bypass the official communication channels and amplify their own message. From the Arab Spring revolutions, to the #MeToo, #BlackLivesMatter, and climate change #FridaysForFuture movements, people have shared information online and organized their communities in a way that has brought political, social, and cultural change in the offline world.

Enter COVID-19. In 2020, pandemic-related restrictions worldwide turned digital spaces into new meeting places for many of us, whether to get information about the pandemic through social media or connect with friends and families through video chat apps. Online interactive formats like Zoom, BigBlueButton, and Skype offered alternatives to dominant in-person work and education.

It is therefore fair to say that digital and offline are not two separate worlds but rather components of the same world we all inhabit. In this spirit, in 2011, the United Nations declared internet access to be a basic human right.

Yet most content on the internet is in a few majority languages such as Arabic, Chinese, English, French, German, Indonesian/Malaysian, Japanese, Portuguese, Russian, and Spanish.[2] In 2020, an Indian Microsoft team was tasked with identifying which languages are found on the internet and which are digitally absent.[3] The study categorizes languages into five groups:

- 88 percent of the world's languages have virtually no internet presence and no language technologies at all. This represents 1 billion speakers who speak languages like Bora, Dahalo, Popoloca, Wallisian, and Warlpiri.

- 9 percent of languages are scraping by in the digital space. These are spoken by 1 billion speakers in total, including languages like Bhojpuri, Cherokee, Diné (Navajo), Fijian, and Greenlandic.

- Less than 1 percent of the world's languages have some internet presence. These are spoken by 300 million people and include languages like Irish, Konkani, Lao, Maltese, and Zulu.

- 1 percent of languages have a strong internet presence but still have few digital language resources. These are spoken by over 1 billion people including languages like Afrikaans, Cebuano, Hebrew, Indonesian, and Ukrainian.

- Less than 1 percent of languages have a clear potential for development in the digital world. These are spoken by 1.6 billion people and include big national languages like Dutch, Hungarian, Korean, Russian, and Vietnamese.

- Finally, only 0.28 percent of languages have a dominant online presence and enjoy industrial and government investments to develop digital technologies. They are spoken by 2.5 billion people in total including languages like English, French, German, Japanese, and Spanish.

The greatest potential for a multilingual internet that includes endangered languages comes from social media. These digital platforms offer informal spaces where the rules can be freely (re)written by users. Because digital communication supports video in addition to text, it is a powerful tool for Deaf people to use sign languages and people who don't read or write to use spoken languages only. People can additionally write in any of the languages they know. Does that language have an official script? Great. Does it not? That's fine too; people seem to be happy to improvise. Who's there to stop them?

For example, I noticed that in the past five years, speakers of Pomak, a minoritized Slavic language in Greece, are making liberal use of Greek and Latin scripts to text on their smartphones or social media. This is a marked change from the early internet years when Pomaks felt they had to write in the languages they were taught at school (Greek and Turkish) but not in their first language, Pomak.

But is it possible to record a message in Pomak and have it instantly transcribed by a speech-to-text tool on one's smartphone like one can do in Greek and Turkish? The answer is . . . not yet. Read the next section to find out more about these technical limitations and what specialists can do to fix them.

## The Tech behind Our Digital Experiences

Our cell phones, tablets, and computers use various technologies to process human languages; we refer to these technologies using the umbrella term *natural language processing* or simply *NLP*. NLP brings together computer scientists, linguists, statisticians, and software engineers, among others who develop technologies that reach billions of people worldwide.

It is needed for many of the services we enjoy when using high-resource languages. In practice, what can NLP do for you today? NLP is behind your searches on the internet; in technical terms, these tasks are known as *question answering*. It is behind translations from one language to another; these tasks are known as *machine translation*. And NLP is behind car navigation systems or your interactions with virtual assistants like Siri and Google Home; these tasks are known as *text to speech*.

Lack of NLP tools has an additional range of real-life consequences. You may be familiar with content moderation on the internet. If so, you know that it is a notoriously difficult task that requires thousands of human moderators going through texts and images and making thousands of decisions daily about what is breaking the law and should thus be removed from the internet. NLP can offer critical assistance with this huge task. When languages are not supported by NLP, predictably, content moderation lags behind.

For example, two Rwandan researchers in international law and conflict management, Felix Ndahinda and Aggée Mugabe, found that social media hate speech during the armed conflict in the Democratic Republic of the Congo escaped moderating policies because most languages are not automatically processed.[4] So even though Lingala, a Bantu language spoken by millions of people, was included in Google Translate in 2022, smaller Bantu languages like Kibembe and Kifuliiru are yet to be integrated.

Big tech companies, aware of these shortcomings, are making efforts to expand their machine translation offers in multiple languages. In 2022, for instance, Google Translate integrated twenty-four additional languages, including some Indigenous languages like Aymara, Guaraní, and Quechua.[5] Since Google favors languages with a sizable number of potential users, these languages have large numbers of speakers.

Researchers assessing priorities for NLP development, however, suggest that we should go beyond purely demographic criteria, which end up supporting languages that are already richly resourced. Instead, why not prioritize low-resourced languages that are used by large numbers of speakers like Amharic, Bambara, Bengali, Kurdish, Oromo, Thai, Urdu, and Yoruba? Additional focus should be put on Indigenous and endangered languages that have virtually zero NLP tools like Aimele, Itelmen, North Saami, and Warlpiri.[6]

Several initiatives are seeking to fill this digital gap and empower Indigenous language users through language technologies. This starts by offering basic access to keyboards or transliteration tools that can handle various writing systems. It goes further by supporting web searches in different languages. One pioneer community-driven Firefox initiative supports a few Indigenous languages like Nahuatl and Triqui spoken in Mexico.[7]

Rather than tech companies and institutions deciding single-handedly which projects are needed, community-driven projects are increasingly taking the lead, clearly articulating their needs, and assessing potential harms.

Jennyfer Lawrence Taylor, a specialist in human-computer interaction, together with the Wujal Wujal Aboriginal Shire Council and community in Australia, explored how participatory design practices could support their efforts to keep their language strong by developing specifically designed technologies. The result was the Crocodile Language Friend, a talking soft toy that was paired with a web application to support children and their families in using their language, Kuku Yalanji.[8]

Another project, funded by the National Research Council of Canada, aims to develop software together with Indigenous communities in Canada.[9] For example, when you write a text on your smartphone in English, you benefit from predictive text suggestions. Let's say you start by typing "good morning"; the system can then suggest "mom" based on your previous usage. The project seeks to make this option available for the Indigenous languages of Canada.

NLP tools can also support language learning and therefore play a role in language reclamation. Second language learners, for instance, can rely on interactive read-along audiobooks where they follow the words one by one as they are highlighted by the software. (Re)learners of languages with complex verb morphology can greatly benefit from verb conjugators too. In collaboration with an adult immersion school in Ontario, a verb conjugator is now available for Kanien'kéha (also known as Mohawk), a language with fourteen stand-alone pronouns and seventy-two pronouns that are bound to the verb and result in thousands of possible conjugations.[10]

Other digital options are available to promote literacy in endangered languages. One exciting option is Story Weaver, an open-source digital platform from Pratham Books that makes it possible to create and access storybooks in any language. In 2021, the Endless Oaxaca Multilingual Project in collaboration with Story Weaver and several local collectives launched a Translation Marathon that led to the creation of more than 150 storybooks in twenty-five of the languages spoken in Oaxaca.[11]

The next section introduces another way in which digital formats can support language reclamation movements: digital language archives.

## Endangered Language Archives Go Digital

Spoken and signed languages are "ephemeral repertoire(s) of embodied practice and knowledge," like dancing, sports, and rituals.[12] How can this knowledge be preserved for future generations?

You probably think of written records as the best long-term solution. Yet the best technology humans have ever invented is the oral tradition. Did you know that Indigenous stories relate human experiences and observations of natural events that can go as far as the end of the last Ice Age, some twenty thousand years ago![13] I don't think we know of a better technology.

But for this ancient knowledge to be preserved across thousands of generations, cultural and language transmission need to be uninterrupted. As you have learned in this book, this is frequently no longer the case. Language documentation thus aims to transform these ephemeral repertoires into enduring materials that can be archived, whether in the form of written texts or audio and video recordings.

At present, affordable mobile technology makes it easier for many communities to self-document their languages. Welcome to the new world of mobile documentation or *mdocumentation*! In one such project, Nubian heritage language learners took over the task of documenting their heritage language after following a language documentation training delivered by the School of Oriental and African Studies along with the Nubian Languages and Culture Project.[14] Keep in mind, however, that such options are not available to remote communities that lack access to landline and mobile internet connections. This was still the case in the late 2000s in the community of Santa María Ixcatlán in Mexico, where I collaborated to document Xhwani (Ixcatec).

Once language recordings have been made, how can one store and preserve them in the long run? When I started making recordings of Nashta, the language of my ancestors, I used minidiscs (remember those?). From minidiscs I moved on to CD-ROMs. Please, tell me if your

At present, affordable mobile technology makes it easier for many communities to self-document their languages.

computer can still read CD-ROMs, let alone minidiscs. The answer is most likely *no*. The ultrahype technology of a given moment in time becomes obsolete one decade later. So if I store minidiscs in my office closet, chances are I'm not really helping with archiving since as the years go by the format becomes obsolete and transfer to new formats more challenging. I've also heard of horror stories where colleagues stored their audiotapes at home, and when they passed away, their descendants unwittingly threw them away.

Lesson number one: if you are in possession of recordings of an endangered language, then a digital archive is probably the best option. I was lucky to have access to a digital archive where I could just upload my Nashta recordings in a Dropbox-like fashion. Selected data are now freely available on the Pangloss Collection (see box), but even the raw data are stored in a long-term perspective with restricted access.

I once opened my personal storage space in this archive and listened to a recording I forgot I even made (twenty years is a long time). I panicked: someone had hacked my space and added recordings I didn't make so maybe I lost some! Luckily, each recording was accompanied by information about when and where it was made, and which language was recorded by which speaker and so on. Lesson number two: the information related to your recordings is not a luxury. This is what we refer to as *metadata*. You may remember who you recorded, which language they used and when, and where you recorded them for a while, but trust me, this information is not going to be stored in your long-term memory.

To summarize: digital archives aim to preserve materials in the most up-to-date technology and facilitate access along with relevant information to identify their contents.

Digital archives for endangered languages started seeing the light of day as computers and the internet became popular. In 2000, the German Volkswagen Foundation set up a program called Documentation of Endangered Languages. The resulting language archive is hosted by the Max Planck Institute in Nijmegen, Netherlands, and contains more than a hundred languages.[15]

In 2002, a nonprofit foundation called Arcadia provided special funds for the documentation of endangered languages in the United Kingdom, the Endangered Languages Documentation Programme, in partnership with the School of Oriental and African Studies, and since 2021, the Berlin Brandenburgische Akademie der Wissenschaften in Germany. The resulting Endangered Languages Archive comprises recordings of more than five hundred languages from seventy countries.[16]

In addition to these archives with worldwide scope, many regional language archives exist. The Archive of the

Indigenous Languages of Latin America, hosted at the University of Texas at Austin in the United States, the Pacific and Regional Archive for Digital Sources in Endangered Cultures, an Australian archive with over thirteen hundred languages mainly from the Pacific area, and the Emilio Goeldi Paraense Museum archive of the languages of Brazil are among such great examples.[17]

---

**Visit the Pangloss Collection**

The Pangloss Collection (pangloss.cnrs.fr) was launched at my research unit (LaCiTO) in the 1990s.[18] It houses audio and video recordings made with speakers of endangered languages and languages spoken by few people. Pangloss means "all languages" and derives from the Greek *pan*, meaning "all," and *glossa*, meaning "language." The collection is the result of more than twenty years of work by researchers from various institutions and software engineers at the CNRS. Most of the recordings are traditional stories, but there are also dialogues between speakers, riddles, jokes, some lists of words, and song recordings.

The collection has grown over the years. Today, it contains approximately eight hundred hours of audio recordings in more than 170 languages.

You will enjoy the melodies and sounds that differ from those of languages that we are accustomed to hearing. But you will not understand much just by listening, and that is why linguists, in collaboration with the speakers of these languages, have prepared transcriptions and translations. To do so, it was first necessary to understand how the grammars of these languages work, and this information is also available in what is called word-for-word transliteration, where each word is accompanied by grammatical information that can be very different from that of English. Half of the recordings are transcribed and annotated, allowing visitors to understand what they are hearing and discover the grammar of the language. Recordings are stored along with related information such as who the speakers are, and where and when the recordings were made.

Unique recordings in the collection are those of the Ubykh language, a Caucasian language that is no longer spoken since the death of Tevfik Esenç. Esenç knew the importance of documenting Ubykh and collaborated with French linguist Georges Dumezil in the 1960s. Recordings made at the time are now available in the Pangloss Collection with transcriptions and translations. Ubykh is a well-known language among linguists because of its seventy consonants, whereas French, for example, has twenty. The use of a different consonant is sometimes enough to change the meaning of a word, as, for instance, in the English *cat* and *hat*, where the only difference is in the initial sounds /k/ and /h/. In the same way, mastering the seventy consonants of Ubykh was necessary to be understood.

Pangloss offers easy access to data by using a persistent Digital Object Identifier for each resource and supports importing the complete record for the resource into reference management tools like Zotero. A script is also available to batch download annotations and audio files—enable the "professional" version of the website on your browser and then click on "tools."

The Pangloss Collection is stored digitally thanks to a French public service, Digital Humanities, that preserves data for as long as possible (and in any case, more than thirty years) and guarantees a high level of data security. Pangloss is also a member of the international Digital Endangered Languages and Music Archives Network.

## Indigenous Data Sovereignty

Legal authorizations to record, store, and access language data are complex and vary with different national legislations worldwide. A comprehensive framework is defined within the European Union General Data Protection Regulation.

Typically, before any recording session, recorded oral or written consent is given by the adult participants in the session. For children, this agreement is provided by their caregivers. The consent is carefully crafted by the researchers and approved by their institutional ethics review board. Consent forms include, among other details, clear mention of the protection of speakers' and signers' identities, whether the participant gives permission or not for the open access of the recordings and their transcriptions, and anonymization preferences. Remember that while I may not want my name to become public in a random recording of me speaking Greek, language keepers are carriers of precious knowledge and may be proud to have their name associated with a recording and claim authorship for the performance of an oral tradition story.

In agreement with these consents, endangered language archives offer various types of data access ranging from access to all internet users to subscribers only. Access can also be differentially provided to speakers and signers or members of the community and other communities as well as teachers and researchers.

Even though digital language archives offer viable long-term options, the preservation of endangered language archives outside the community of origin and beyond its control raises additional ethical questions. Lesley Woods, a Ngiyampaa person and PhD candidate in Australia, investigates how Indigenous peoples lost control over the cultural and language knowledge that was collected by academic researchers in the past.[19] Copyright laws in Australia (and elsewhere) are by default giving copyright to the person who presses the button on the recorder. This is how researchers who documented Australian languages over the years automatically became the legal owners of the recordings while language users and communities were required to ask permission to access these materials. When these researchers passed away, materials that were not copyrighted in the public domain were transferred as part of their inheritance, removing these recordings twice from the original community.

I witnessed a similar case with Xhwani (Ixcatec), a language that is currently spoken in Mexico by a handful of people. In 1950, Doroteo Jiménez, a speaker of Xhwani, collaborated with Mexican linguist María Teresa Fernández de Miranda to produce the first dictionary and associated texts in Xhwani. When both Jiménez and Fernández de Miranda passed away, the recordings of their working sessions, which were made at the National Museum of Anthropology in Mexico City, landed in the University of

Chicago Digital Media Archive. The archive did a great job at preventing the loss of the data and updating the recordings in digital formats. But think of how strange it is that the inheritance of the Ixcatec community now belongs to an institution in the United States that holds the copyright.

Over the past two decades, it has therefore become clear that there is an urgent need for the recognition and protection of Indigenous data rights. This is known as Indigenous Data Sovereignty and applies to all types of data, both human (such as linguistic, anthropological, and genomic) and nonhuman (such as minerals, plants, animals, artifacts, and so on).

In 2010, the UN Convention on Biological Diversity adopted the Nagoya Protocol, which offers legislation about access to resources and data from and about Indigenous communities along with their lands, waters, and species. Even though the Nagoya Protocol is not signed by all countries that are home to Indigenous peoples, it offers important guidance for research policies. What does this entail?

Under the Indigenous Data Sovereignty rights, blanket open science policies promoting Findable, Accessible, Interoperable, and Reusable (FAIR) principles for data need to be adjusted. As anthropologist Cori Hayden notes in her book *When Nature Goes Public*, the establishment of public domains might seem like progress, but at the same time disrupts the understanding that local and Indigenous communities have a claim on Indigenous or local knowledge.[20] To remedy this, in 2019, the Global Indigenous Data Alliance added a set of principles that focus on Collective benefit, Authority to control, Responsibility, and Ethics (CARE) in Indigenous data governance.[21]

While it is admittedly difficult for individual speakers and signers to negotiate the CARE principles and their implementation, it is easier for language community associations to negotiate with academic institutions and private foundations on a more equal footing. In *Something's Gotta Change*, Woods is thus advocating for the implementation of agreements between universities and communities to help communities keep control of their cultural and linguistic heritage.[22]

An illustration of the various forms that Indigenous Data Sovereignty can take comes from Aotearoa New Zealand. In 2018, a small nonprofit Māori organization, Te Hiku Media, organized a competition to record as many te reo Māori speakers as it could. The result was an impressive collection of three hundred hours of language recordings with associated annotations. In the spirit of Indigenous Data Sovereignty, the Māori people declined offers from tech to buy their language data sets and chose instead to develop automatic speech recognition and speech-to-text transcription on their own.[23] Recall that this is the kind of NLP technology that will one day allow te reo Māori speakers to record their voice on a smartphone and get the message accurately transcribed.

This te reo Māori–led initiative offers a sustainable alternative to the current big tech models that scrape data from the internet to develop tools that corporations can later sell for profit to te reo Māori speakers. Te Hiku Media operates instead under the Kaitiakitanga License that treats data with respect, like one would treat a family member. Under this license, Te Hiku Media does not claim ownership of the data but rather acts as a custodian, looking after the data, respecting the people the data came from, and striving for the technologies based on the data to benefit the entire community.[24]

But what happens with ownership rights that predate Indigenous Data Sovereignty agreements? One path that institutions are currently taking is known as *rematriation*. This is not a typo. While repatriation is rooted in Western and/or European concepts of ownership and property in which Indigenous peoples need to gain permission to access their own cultural inheritance, rematriation is shifting the focus to prioritize what Indigenous peoples need and act in agreement with their values.[25] Stay tuned and advocate for rematriation whenever you can.

**Key Takeaways**

• Most content on the internet is in a few global and official state languages. Endangered languages are virtually absent from the digital space.

• Several community-driven initiatives are seeking to fill this digital gap and empower Indigenous language users through language technologies.

• Digital language archives are aiming to preserve recordings of endangered languages for the next generations and make them available to the current ones.

• In an Indigenous Data Sovereignty perspective, language data are subject to the laws and governance of the nation or community from which they are collected.

• CARE principles focus on collective benefit, the authority to control languages, responsibility, and ethics in Indigenous data governance.

# MULTILINGUALISM AS RESOLUTION

So that's, in a nutshell, the arc of my relationship with my native language, Haitian Creole. From basically self-hatred, denial, to now—let's call it—self-love and having language blossom, not just for me, but for the whole nation.

—Michel DeGraff, "What Are Creole Languages, Anyway?," *Speaking of Us* (podcast)

## Being Multilingual

I grew up in the Balkans, an area in southeastern Europe delimited to the north by the Danube River and to the south by the Mediterranean Sea. More than a geographic area, the Balkans form a sociopolitical and cultural area shaped by a centuries-long common history within the

Byzantine Empire from the fourth to the fifteenth century, and then within the Ottoman Empire from the fifteenth to the early twentieth century. We find speakers of two language families: Turkic and Indo-European, represented by different language groupings like Albanian, Armenic, Greek, Indic, Romance, and Slavic.

In the Balkans, multilingualism was widespread and constant over time. People would share knowledge of the two major languages of the empires, Greek and Turkish, that they used for trade, administration, and religion. One outcome was that speakers of different first languages would use the same words. Today, we still know and use informal conversational Turkish words like *hayde*, meaning "let's go," and *tamam*, meaning "OK!," no matter what our first language is and whether we also speak Turkish or not.

In addition, Balkan people would often form linguistically mixed households and reside in linguistically mixed localities. Rather than shifting altogether to a single shared language, people would use these various languages at home and in the community. Over time, bilingual individuals would spontaneously combine the grammars of the languages they spoke. Because there were no strong prescriptive norms, the grammars of these languages grew to be increasingly alike. When this process is repeated multiple times between different pairs of languages, then the languages in this multilingual area end up having a partly shared grammar and lexicon. Linguists refer to this outcome as a *linguistic area*.

The Balkan linguistic area offers an excellent illustration of this phenomenon as it includes language groupings that are used both within and outside the Balkans.[1] Scholars can, for instance, showcase how most Slavic languages in the Balkans have developed definite articles (that follow the nominals) while Slavic languages at the periphery or outside the Balkans haven't. In addition, scholars can trace the grammatical changes across the centuries thanks to ample written records demonstrating how language-specific processes emerge and are reinforced due to language contact; such well-documented phenomena are the loss of infinitives and cases.[2]

This intense multilingual situation is not unique to the Balkans. In fact, multilingual models were common across the world and led to the formation of linguistic areas from Oceania and Indigenous Australia, to Mesoamerica and North America, the Amazon, Central and South Asia, and West and South Africa.

For example, in the precolonial cultural space of Mapungubwe in southern Africa, speakers of Khoisan, Nguni, and Sotho languages sustained economic and social relations, strengthened by intermarriages. Like in the Balkans, the individuals in these groups didn't adopt a single language but used multiple languages instead.

South African linguist Leketi Makalela reports a discussion with an Elder that illustrates this intricate relationship: "We used to live with everyone around us. So, we learned to talk to each other. You can see our surnames. There are the Mabundas, Sathekges, Mpheti, which are all different languages. But everyone knew each other's languages. My relatives are from many different groups and we don't see ourselves as different. The whole of Bushbuckridge area is called Mapulaneng because we are mixed."[3]

Makalela captures this kind of multilingual ideology in South Africa through the term *ubuntu translanguaging*. The concept of *ubuntu* reflects the worldview whereby the individual and collective are interconnected. Makalela suggests that languages are likewise interdependent, without clear boundaries in their usage. This contrasts with the colonial construction of African "tribes" understood as naturalized and linguistically homogeneous units—a view that prevails in much of the modern anthropological and linguistic theorizing of African languages and people.[4]

For the future of endangered languages, multilingual perspectives from the Global South like ubuntu translanguaging are a game changer. They offer a frame in which speakers and signers no longer need to choose between a majority and an Indigenous, minoritized, or endangered language but instead can draw on multiple languages depending on their needs.

What could these needs be? They are of course inter-person communication needs, but they also represent much deeper connections with the ancestors. To illustrate this spiritual connection, let me recount the experience of the Koryaks in far eastern Siberia. The Koryaks no longer use their ancestral language, Koryak, and have shifted to Russian in daily life. Koryaks traditionally lived in villages along the coast, where they relied on fishing or were reindeer herders and had to move across the tundra with the seasons. Today when the Koryaks return to their ancestral lands, they often report experiencing a sleep paralysis. In the middle of the night, they wake up with something resembling an anxiety crisis. They can then see shadows of people in the dark, but they are unable to move to protect themselves from them. To make these visions cease, Koryaks must ask them to "go away" in their ancestral language, Koryak. It appears that the Koryak language alone can open communication with the world of dreams.[5] For a people that has traditionally practiced shamanism, the spiritual connection to the Koryak language can't easily be replaced by Russian.

Such a strong connection to the language of the ancestors is common across the world. When asked to describe her language profile, Nancy Ngalmindjalmag, a Warruwi Elder from Australia, mentions eight languages.[6]

Mawng is her father's language, which she learned as a child, and it is today spoken by about 300 people. Where

Nancy Ngalmindjalmag lives, the father's language is linked to the land in a way that you don't only inherit and own your father's land but you inherit and own your father's language too. You may use this language or not, yet you still *own the language*.

More generally, in Indigenous Australia, the connection between language and land is a profound one. When they traveled, Indigenous people in Australia were expected to know the language of the land they would visit. So when someone would visit another land, they would know this language well enough to understand it even if they couldn't speak it. The conversation was frequently conducted in two languages, with each person speaking their own language and understanding the other person's language.

The second language that Nancy Ngalmindjalmag cites is Kunwinjku. This is her mother's language, which she also learned as a child. Kunwinjku is used today by about one thousand people.

Djambarrpuyngu is her husband's paternal language. It is one variety of Yolngu-matha, a language with up to 5,000 speakers. Nancy Ngalmindjalmag typically speaks her own father's language, Mawng, to her husband, and he responds in Yolngu-matha.

Standard Australian English is the language Nancy Ngalmindjalmag used when working in the regional capital, Darwin.

Nancy Ngalmindjalmag also mentions Kunbarlang and Iwaidja. These are two languages that were spoken in neighboring lands. Because there were many intermarriages, Kunbarlang and Iwaidja were spoken by many of the ancestors of today's Mawng speakers. Currently, however, Kunbarlang and Iwaidja are known by fewer than 30 people each.

Na-kara (spoken by 50 people) and Ndjébbana (spoken by 250 people) are two more languages that Nancy Ngalmindjalmag knows, although she mentions that she uses them to a lesser extent.

Are you impressed? You can now write down the languages you use and understand to create your own language profile. You might impress yourself! But you may also come from a monolingual background. For example, just 20 percent of the US population speaks a language other than English at home and 20 percent learn another language at school.[7]


## Bilingualism in the Mind and Brain

People living in monolingual settings often understand bilingualism as an ideal state where one person knows and uses two languages in the exact way two monolinguals do. This is fiction. Our minds are constantly adapting to our complex language experiences whether we use a single language or multiple ones.[8]

Let's see how this works by examining language production.[9] The standard model of language production applies to spoken, sign, and written language production and can apply to monolingual, bilingual, and multilingual language users.

According to the standard model, a language user starts by (partly) forming a nonlinguistic message, taking into consideration the semantic meaning as well as contextual and pragmatic factors. Nonetheless, this nonlinguistic message is already influenced by the characteristics of the language in which it will be expressed, so that the language user needs to think of tense if the language encodes tense and so on.

Then the mind activates the relevant lexical items that are stored in the mental lexicon. Once the appropriate lexical items are selected, the mind gains access to their semantic, morphological, and syntactic properties and encodes them into sentences. Lexical items are stored in a single system and have multiple links with one another, with some items having direct links with others. During lexical selection, language users activate some words while inhibiting other semantically related words of the same syntactic category. For example, if you want to say, sign, or write "I love pigeons," you will need to activate the target noun *pigeons* more than the semantically related noun *doves* (the latter will also be activated, but to a lesser extent).

Your next task is to put in order and establish the syntactic connections of these enriched lexical items; you decide which one is the subject, and which one is the object, based on how the language encodes these functions. In the sentence "I love pigeons," you will place the object *pigeons* after the verb *love* and the subject pronoun *I* before it.

Finally, the mind retrieves and encodes the different word forms and converts them into spoken or manual actions, activating a complex set of muscles in order to speak, sign, or write.

All of this happens superfast; we produce about two words in a second, taking quick turns with our interlocutor every two to three hundred milliseconds!

Bilinguals go through the same language production process. The difference is that they additionally need to select the language from which to draw the lexicon, grammar, and phonology; this is managed by a mechanism known as *language control*. It is still unclear whether the lexical items of a bilingual individual are stored in a single system or two different subsystems. Language subsystems are activated based on the interactional context and intended meaning. Each language subsystem has different activation thresholds; this is different from proficiency and changes over time.

I have spent years using French, for instance, so it is easier to activate French even though Greek is the language I learned first as a child and used for a large part of my life. This will become apparent in a verbal fluency test, where people are asked to cite as many words as fast as they can. When I do this task while in France, I cite more words and faster in French (the more activated language at that specific time in my life) than in Greek. This doesn't mean that I don't know the words in Greek; they just come to mind more slowly because I'm not using them as much as I use the French words.

Even though the process of speech production is similar for monolinguals and bilinguals, bilinguals typically have larger stocks of words in their minds. I have a large lexical stock that includes the same words in English, French, and Greek. In some cases, however, I only have words in some of these languages; for example, to talk about linguistics, I know more technical terms in English than in French or Greek. Bilinguals (and multilinguals) therefore need slightly more time to select and retrieve a word because they must search for it in a larger stock of words and inhibit more competitors; this is known as the *bilingual disadvantage* (spoiler: there is also a bilingual advantage; read on to the next section).

The ability to retrieve a given word constantly changes for monolinguals and bilinguals alike, depending on how we slept last night, how busy our mind is, how often we use a word, or when we last used that specific word. After a holiday break, I take more time to retrieve certain technical terms. This effect doesn't last more than a couple of days, and these technical words quickly come to mind once again.

Overall, the human mind adapts to the kind of language interactions one has most frequently. If you often interact with monolinguals, then the two stocks of words in your mind will tend to remain separate. If you often interact with bilinguals and they accept that you can draw words from the entirety of your shared lexical stock, then the two languages in your mind will tend to be connected.

In fact, drawing on whatever words are most available without language separation is what the human mind prefers. Many studies show that both lexicons and grammars are constantly active in the bilingual mind, whether during language comprehension or production. I have noticed that sometimes when I'm tired, a word from one language (let's say Greek) may pop up in a conversation even though I know that my French-speaking interlocutor (who doesn't speak Greek) will not understand it. My selection and inhibition mechanism has just failed me, indicating that all the languages I know are active in my mind. Even when language users try to keep languages separate in conversation, these languages share the same neural networks.[10] This physiological overlap in the brain may reflect the tendency of the grammars and lexicons of bilinguals to converge over time, as we know happened in the Balkans.

It follows that if we could use both languages at the same time, we would do so. In fact, this is exactly what people who use languages in two different modalities do. It is common for the hearing children of Deaf parents to use *at the same time* a sign language, relying on manual and facial signs, along with a spoken language.[11] It doesn't mean that they will utter each word in the two languages, like professional interpreters must do, but rather they will draw several words and grammar from both languages even when there is a mismatch between the two grammars.

Let me give one more example from the study of cognitive costs related to language switching. Many studies have found that people who aren't used to alternating from one language to another take a few milliseconds more to complete a bilingual task than a task in a single language. In contrast, when switching between languages is the default way of communicating, then people have little to no additional delay when they complete the bilingual task as compared to the task in a single language.

To test this, we collaborated with Muslim Roma people in the Balkans who have been using Turkish for trade since the Ottoman times and Romani for in-group communication. Over time, some Romani groups started using the two languages in their in-group conversations in such a way that this became their default way of speaking Romani. Today when they speak in this mixed Romani-Turkish way, they use both Romani and Turkish verbs with their respective Romani and Turkish verb grammatical categories. You can see in italics the words from Turkish and in roman those from Romani: "*ep* me ka dikhav kale, me *da səndəm*, me *da* mangav *dineneəm*," which means, "Am I *always* the one to look after them? I'm *tired* of it! Me *too*, I want to *rest*."

This way of mixing two languages is something that we rarely see among bilinguals in other parts of the world. People who use two languages typically alternate between the two languages in longer stretches (*code switching*) or use the verb or noun of one language with the grammar of the other (*borrowing*). For instance, French-English speakers from Canada might code switch from French to English (in italics) as in, "Il a dit que des fois là, quand il marchait là, il marchait *over dead bodies*," which means, "He said that sometimes when he walked, he was walking *over dead bodies*." Or they might borrow and use an English verb with French grammar in an otherwise French sentence: "Puis les parents ont jamais voulu qu'ils la *déplug*," which means, "And the parents never wanted them to *unplug* her."[12]

Going back to our study on Romani-Turkish, we showed Romani-Turkish speakers two pictures on a computer screen and associated them to an audio sentence that was related in meaning to only one of the two pictures. We then asked the participants to press a key on the laptop to indicate the correct picture. The computer program measured the time it took each participant to press the key when they listened to a mixed Romani-Turkish sentence as compared to one that only contained Turkish words and grammar. We found that the participants responded faster for the mixed Romani-Turkish sentences only when these followed the exact language-mixing rules that they used in their language community.[13] Our experimental study therefore confirms that language experience matters and that the mind adapts to it and processes fastest the most familiar language uses.

The effects of varied language experiences can also be seen in the brain. Studies in neurolinguistics indicate that brain structure and connectivity are shaped depending on the way people use language. The brains of immersed bilinguals, who learned two languages one after the other, differ from the brains of bilinguals who learned two languages at the same time or in a nonimmersive way, and from the brains of multilinguals who learned more than two languages.

Neurolinguist Christos Pliatsikas summarizes these findings and identifies three different stages in second language learning.[14] During the first stage, there is an immediate effect of learning an additional language in local cortical gray matter volume. Then with time and as experience with this language increases, the effect in gray matter volume is replaced by white matter (which is responsible for the connectivity between neurons) and subcortical restructuring. Brain restructuring does not only depend on the amount of experience one has in learning an additional language but also on the experience one has in

The effects of varied language experiences can also be seen in the brain.

keeping languages separate or alternating between these languages in a single conversation as we saw above for the Romani-Turkish speakers.

In fact, a dynamic understanding of how our brains work goes beyond language use. An illustration I like comes from research conducted with trainee London taxi drivers who must take a final exam consisting of, among other things, memorizing the map of London. The researchers found that the brain of the trainees who were successful in the final exam differed from the brain of the trainees who failed the exam. The brain of the successful candidates showed increased gray matter in the hippocampus and changes in memory profile whereas the brain of those who failed did not exhibit these changes.[15]

The constant training one gets when using two languages seems to come with a few advantages that go beyond language. Go to the next section to learn more about this.

## Praise for Bilingualism

"Why Bilinguals Are Smarter" is the kind of pop-science piece you are likely to read nowadays. This, however, was not the belief for much of the twentieth century. Quite the opposite. I remember that as recently as the 1980s, I had to convince my parents to allow me to learn English in addition to French because teachers told them it would be confusing. Even today I keep hearing from parents around me that they don't want to use two languages with their child, considering that it's best for them to properly learn one language first before learning a second language, and, much later, a third one.

This prejudice against bilingualism has its roots in early twentieth-century Western science. At the time, measurements of intelligence were common as part of the eugenics movement, and some studies investigated whether bilingualism made you smarter. The early studies regularly reported that monolinguals were smarter than bilinguals, and these recurrent findings ended up stigmatizing individuals and groups that deviated from this monolingual ideal.

For example, one study from Wales in 1923 concludes that "monoglot children in rural districts in Wales show a considerable superiority over bilingual children in the same districts when tested by the Binet scale of intelligence," "university students coming from rural areas in Wales show the same differentiation in a test of intelligence," and "the greatest influence on the mental confusion occurring in bilingualism is exerted by the language used by bilingual children in their play and in their free association with youthful companions when that language is not also that in which they are first taught at school."[16] Remember how pupils around the world were punished for using their ancestral language at school? This kind of research probably had something to do with it.

It was not until the 1960s that the stigmatization of bilingualism was successfully challenged. In one influential study, Elizabeth Peal and Wallace E. Lambert of McGill University found that bilingual children in Quebec outperformed monolingual children in the verbal and nonverbal intelligence tests of the times.[17] The authors explained that bilingual children must have greater mental flexibility because of the constant practice in managing two languages.

Scientists have now solidly established that bilingual children are not more prone to learning delays or language disorders than monolingual children.[18] Studies indicate that while bilingualism may initially present a challenge for children, as they memorize and process twice as much information as monolinguals, it quickly enhances their memory skills, including their nonverbal working memory. Similarly, learning to select and inhibit different languages is a skill that transfers to nonverbal tasks like inhibiting an incorrect response. This is the *bilingual advantage*.

Moreover, scientists are increasingly drawing attention to the value of bilingualism for ensuring connection to family culture and history and offering additional opportunities in employment. Bilingual children also appear to be more attuned to other people's perspectives, thoughts, and intentions thanks to the rich experience they gain when interacting with various groups of people that use different languages.

In addition, researchers are unveiling the bilingual advantage among older adults. For example, researchers found that brain plasticity due to the use of more than one language throughout the life span is associated with better resistance to age-related gray matter loss in older age, the *brain reserve*. Older bilinguals also exhibit some *cognitive reserve*, which translates into better executive control for the three major functions: inhibition, attention switching, and working memory. Impressively, some studies find that bilingualism delays the onset of Alzheimer's by four to five years. In an aging world, a soft remedy like bilingual practice throughout life is a huge asset to our health systems.[19]

## Embracing the Use of Multiple Languages

Societies regularly update their norms, and we could currently be going through such a transformational moment. In 2021, a team of scholars in applied linguistics published a manifesto that proposes to introduce translanguaging approaches in formal education.[20] In this approach, educators welcome and value whatever language experiences children bring to school, without the separation and social stigmatization of named institutionalized languages.

What does this mean in practice? In their manifesto, Ofelia García and her colleagues relate their experience with a Mexican American girl, Margarita, born in the United States. Margarita's language skills were assessed to decide whether she would join an English-as-a-second-language program or the more advanced dual language bilingual program. Such tests rely on an understanding of languages as distinct units and assess proficiency separately in each. In this case, the assessment was based on a task in which Margarita was asked to describe some pictures. One picture showed a woman making cookies at home. For the assessment, if Margarita used the word *dough* in addition to the word *cookie*, she would gain more points since *dough* is considered more academic than *cookie*. Margarita adequately described the picture using the word *cookies*, but didn't use the word *dough* in doing so, and thus didn't get those extra points. The translanguaging approach notes that Margarita grew up in a home where they would regularly make *tortillas* with *masa*. She therefore didn't know the word *dough*, although she would have offered the word *masa* had she been shown a picture of someone making tortillas. As a result, Margarita joined the English-as-a-second-language program, which didn't adequately reflect her language skills.

The translanguaging approach not only invites us to challenge the monolingual norm but also reconceptualize language as *languaging*, a dynamic and heterogeneous process. Rather than aiming for two perfectly separate languages, current models consider that people draw on words and grammatical structures depending on the real-world actions that they perform, as illustrated by Margarita. This is not just a more accurate depiction of language use; it offers a more flexible and welcoming perspective to language practices in endangered languages.

For example, contemporary te reo Māori speakers regularly combine English words and phrases with te reo Māori words and phrases, while te reo Māori greetings and place-names are now part of New Zealand English. This leads Te Hiku Media to stress the need to develop digital technologies that are not baffled by this kind of real-life language production.[21]

What are the obstacles to such radical change in our monolingual practices and ideologies? As French sociologist Pierre Bourdieu noted, languages are marked means of communication and linked to symbolic power.[22] At a collective level, we are biased against other people's languages or ways of using language only in certain ways: we only discriminate against the languages and ways of using language for groups of people that do not hold power in society. British English pronunciation may be valued in the United States, but other English pronunciations, less so. These biases are so entrenched that they defy objective characterization.

One study, for instance, finds that when participants listened to English sound files associated with the face of a South Asian woman, they judged her speech as "more accented" even though the sound file was in US English. In contrast, when they saw the face of a European American woman, they judged her speech as "less accented" even though the sound file was in Indian English.[23]

In a nutshell, the conservative approach to multiculturalism and multilingualism aimed in the past to build an idealized monolingual nation-state by eradicating other languages. Today the liberal approach invites us to celebrate everyone's cultures and languages based on the assumption that everyone is equal and therefore everyone can freely choose which languages to use. In contrast, the critical approach seeks to unveil the relations of power in society in order to empower discriminated and racialized groups in their struggle for social and language justice.[24]

**Key Takeaways**

• People in many parts of the world were and sometimes still are bilingual or multilingual.

• Being bilingual or multilingual means that you can draw from different languages depending on your communication needs.

• While bilingualism was stigmatized in the past, we now understand its many social and cognitive benefits.

- The multilingual practices of groups of people that are perceived as not holding any power are stigmatized.

- Reembracing traditional multilingual ideologies and practices is one way of keeping our ancestral languages strong.

# CONCLUSION

Tips to Promote Language Diversity

In this book, we have seen that 58 percent of languages are endangered. Like global warming numbers, we may feel overwhelmed by the urgency of language endangerment. This is an understandable reaction to catastrophic news, but the truth is that there is time to reverse the trend and support our language community as well as other ones that wish to strengthen their language.

For example, the 2022 Report on the Status of British Columbia First Nations Languages finds that in addition to ten thousand speakers (representing 7 percent of the Indigenous population), there has been an increase of three thousand Indigenous active learners since 2018.[1] This number includes children who attend recently available immersion language nests and use the language at home, and adults who attend immersion language programs, mentor-apprentice programs, and use online learning tools. Nonetheless, keep in mind that the success of language reclamation can't be reduced to numbers. As we have seen, language reclamation plays a key restorative and protective role for Indigenous communities across the world.[2]

Here are eight ways to promote multilingualism and language diversity, ranging from easy to time intensive:

**Easy**

• Learn about your own ancestral language and which Indigenous, minoritized, and endangered languages were and are used where you live.

• Learn how to greet and thank people in these languages.

• Listen to music in Indigenous and minoritized languages.

• Celebrate Indigenous and minoritized languages and language initiatives on social media.

• Write to your political representatives to ask for support for local Indigenous peoples and minoritized language communities in preserving, revitalizing, and strengthening their languages.

**Time Intensive**

- (Re)connect with your own community and other Indigenous or minoritized communities in your area and learn more about their actions.

- Enroll in language classes or listen to language podcasts.

- Get involved in language documentation as an academic or citizen scientist.

The time to act is now.

# ACKNOWLEDGMENTS

This book offers a synthesis of my understanding of language endangerment that was not only nurtured by reading academic and nonacademic work but also by spending time with many individuals and communities that deserve thanks and credit. I cannot directly name those who live in Greece, as the political situation is unstable.

I am deeply grateful to my mother, my grandparents, and their friends who taught me Nashta.

I extend enormous gratitude to my Pomak friends and language consultants for welcoming me throughout the years in their homes.

I owe a particular debt to the Romani communities of Greece for their massive participation in several of my studies over the years, Romani leader and activist Dalila Gómez in Colombia, and Yolanda Montes and her family in Mexico. I also thank my coauthor and former PhD student Cristian Padure as well as Esteban Acuña Cabanzo, who collaborated with the Romani communities in Romania and Colombia.

Another great debt is owed to the Xhwani speakers who collaborated on the language documentation project (in alphabetical order): Gregorio Hernández García, Cipriano Ramírez Guzmán, Rosalía Ramírez Salazar, Rufina Robles, Patrocinia Salazar, Juliana Salazar Bautista, and

Pedro Salazar Gutiérrez. I am also intensely grateful to the many Ixcatecs who made me and my family feel welcome in Santa María Ixcatlán, Mexico.

Many thanks to Atieh Asgharzadeh and Denis Costaouec for their feedback on earlier drafts of this book, helping me better adapt my writing to a nonspecialist audience.

Thank you to Tanguy Solliec for creating the map in figure 2, as well as Margaret Dunham and Rosalba Putrino for their work on the manuscript.

I am grateful to the three anonymous reviewers who made excellent comments on the proposal, allowing me to refine my thinking, and the other three anonymous reviewers for carefully reading the manuscript and helping me improve its quality. Any errors are, of course, entirely my own.

I also owe thanks to my colleagues and collaborators for providing the intellectually stimulating atmosphere in which I conducted my research. Special thanks to Ignasi-Xavier Adiego Lajara, Pius Wuchu Akumbu, Simon Greenhill, Alexis Michaud, Tatiana Nikitina, Ergin Öpengin, Thomas Pellard, and Maïa Ponsonnet for their suggestions on specific parts of the manuscript.

Finally, I thank Philip Laughlin, Haley Biermann, Virginia Crossman, Cindy Milstein, and Debora Kuan at the MIT Press for their trust in this book and a smooth production process.

# GLOSSARY

**Accent**
A pronunciation that provides clues as to geography, socioeconomic class, education, ethnicity, and first language. We all have an "accent" to someone who belongs to a different social group.

**Attrition (of the first language)**
When a bilingual uses a second language in their everyday life, they may experience loss of some aspects of their first language.

**Bilingual**
A person who understands and/or uses two languages.

**Code switching**
Alternating between languages within a single conversation.

**Creole**
A Creole is a language that emerged in adverse contexts involving slavery and race segregation.

**Digital gap**
The difference between the few languages that are present on the internet and those that are absent from it.

**Dormant language**
A language that has no known language users but is still associated with a community.

**Elder**
An Elder is an Indigenous community member who is valued for their knowledge and teachings.

**Extinct language**
A language that has had no language users for centuries and is not claimed by a community.

**Indigenous**
This is an inclusive term that refers to people who inhabited a territory before the arrival of settlers.

**Indigenous Data Sovereignty**
Data are subject to the laws and governance of the nation from which they are collected.

**Indigenous methodologies**
A framework that is anchored in Indigenous epistemology, theory, and ethics, and involves hearing story and engaging with the community in a respectful and reciprocal relationship.

**Language community**
A community of speakers or signers sharing the same language.

**Language policy**
Initially, a set of activities that a state develops in order to promote and regulate the status of languages. More recently, a combination of individual and group behaviors and beliefs about language.

**Language reclamation**
A holistic framework that not only aims to strengthen a language but also involves community-led cultural and political resurgence.

**Language revitalization**
A frame of actions that aim to reverse language shift and strengthen the use of a community's language.

**Language shift**
When people stop using their first language and start using another socially dominant language, often in a context of discrimination, minoritization, and colonization.

**Linguistic area**
A group of languages that do not belong to the same language group or family but share structural and lexical similarities that result from intensive and extensive bilingualism over time.

**Minoritized language**
A language that has been marginalized, usually through the process of modern nation-state creation.

**Reawakening (a language)**
The process of reclaiming a language that has been dormant.

**Sign language**
Sign languages are used by Deaf people to communicate with other Deaf and hearing people. Signers rely on codified manual signs together with facial expressions, head positions, and body postures.

**Silent speaker**
A person who understands a spoken language but is not comfortable speaking it.

**Translanguaging**
Translanguaging is a term that captures the dynamic nature of language practices and rejects the colonial boundaries of named languages. It has emerged in the domains of applied linguistics and education.

# NOTES

**Chapter 1**

1. Emily M. Bender et al., "On the Dangers of Stochastic Parrots: Can Language Models Be Too Big?," in *Proceedings of the 2021 ACM Conference on Fairness, Accountability, and Transparency* (New York: ACM, 2021), 610–623, https://doi.org/10.1145/3442188.3445922.

2. Stephanie L. King and Vincent M. Janik, "Bottlenose Dolphins Can Use Learned Vocal Labels to Address Each Other," *Proceedings of the National Academy of Sciences of the United States of America* 110, no. 32 (2013): 13216–13221, https://doi.org/10.1073/pnas.1304459110.

3. Angela D. Friederici, *Language in Our Brain: The Origins of a Uniquely Human Capacity* (Cambridge, MA: MIT Press, 2017), https://doi.org/10.7551/mitpress/9780262036924.001.0001.

4. Robert C. Berwick et al., "Songs to Syntax: The Linguistics of Birdsong," *Trends in Cognitive Sciences* 15, no. 3 (March 2011): 113–121, https://doi.org/10.1016/j.tics.2011.01.002.

5. Seweryn Olkowicz et al., "Birds Have Primate-Like Numbers of Neurons in the Forebrain," *Proceedings of the National Academy of Sciences* 113, no. 26 (June 28, 2016): 7255–7260, https://doi.org/10.1073/pnas.1517131113.

6. Christos Pliatsikas, "Understanding Structural Plasticity in the Bilingual Brain: The Dynamic Restructuring Model," *Bilingualism: Language and Cognition* 23, no. 2 (2020): 459–471, https://doi.org/10.1017/S1366728919000130.

7. Mairéad MacSweeney et al., "The Signing Brain: The Neurobiology of Sign Language," *Trends in Cognitive Sciences* 12, no. 11 (November 2008): 432–440, https://doi.org/10.1016/j.tics.2008.07.010; Karen Emmorey, *Language, Cognition, and the Brain: Insights from Sign Language Research* (Milton Park, UK: Taylor and Francis, 2001).

8. Stanislas Dehaene et al., "Illiterate to Literate: Behavioural and Cerebral Changes Induced by Reading Acquisition," *Nature Reviews Neuroscience* 16, no. 4 (April 2015): 234–244, https://doi.org/10.1038/nrn3924.

9. Wesley Y. Leonard, "When Is an 'Extinct Language' Not Extinct? Miami, a Formerly Sleeping Language," in *Sustaining Linguistic Diversity: Endangered and Minority Languages and Language Varieties*, ed. Kendall King et al. (Washington, DC: Georgetown University Press, 2008), 23–34.

10. This figure is based on up-to-date information from Glottolog's Agglomerated Endangerment Status, which brings together information from primary

sources such as Catalogue of Endangered Languages, UNESCO Atlas of the World's Languages in Danger, and Ethnologue. Harald Hammarström et al., *Glottolog 4.7* (Leipzig: Max Planck Institute for Evolutionary Biology, 2022), https://doi.org/10.5281/zenodo.7398962.

11. Hammarström et al., *Glottolog 4.7*.

12. Lyle Campbell and Anna Belew, eds., *Cataloguing the World's Endangered Languages* (London: Routledge, 2018).

13. Julien Meyer, *Whistled Languages: A Worldwide Inquiry on Human Whistled Speech* (Heidelberg: Springer, 2015), https://doi.org/10.1007/978-3-662-45837-2.

14. Umberto Ansaldo and Lisa Lim, "Language Contact in the Asian Region," in *The Routledge Handbook of Language Contact*, ed. Evangelia Adamou and Yaron Matras (London: Routledge, 2020), 434–461.

15. Michel DeGraff, "Toward Racial Justice in Linguistics: The Case of Creole Studies (Response to Charity Hudley et al.)," *Language* 96, no. 4 (2020): e292–e306, https://doi.org/10.1353/lan.2020.0080.

16. Annelies Kusters et al., eds., *Sign Language Ideologies in Practice* (Berlin: De Gruyter, 2020), https://doi.org/10.1515/9781501510090.

17. Attributed to a Bronx high school teacher who attended Max Weinreich's lecture. Max Weinreich, *Der YIVO un di problemen fun undzer tsayt* (New York: Yidisher Visnshaftlekher Institut—Yivo, 1945).

18. "Guidelines for Inclusive Language," Linguistic Society of America, accessed July 10, 2023, https://www.linguisticsociety.org/resource/guidelines-inclusive-language.

19. Patrick McConvell and Felicity Meakins, "Gurindji Kriol: A Mixed Language Emerges from Code-Switching," *Australian Journal of Linguistics* 25, no. 1 (April 2005): 9–30, https://doi.org/10.1080/07268600500110456.

20. Eréndira Calderón, Stefano De Pascale, and Evangelia Adamou, "How to Speak 'Geocentric' in an 'Egocentric' Language: A Multimodal Study among Ngigua-Spanish Bilinguals and Spanish Monolinguals in a Rural Community of Mexico," *Language Sciences* 74 (July 2019): 24–46, https://doi.org/10.1016/j.langsci.2019.04.001.

21. Sinfree Makoni, Cristine Severo, and Ashraf Abdelhay, "Postcolonial Language Policy and Planning and the Limits of the Notion of the Modern State," *Annual Review of Linguistics* 9, no. 1 (January 17, 2023): 483–496, https://doi.org/10.1146/annurev-linguistics-030521-052930.

22. Lise M. Dobrin, "SIL International and the Disciplinary Culture of Linguistics: Introduction," *Language* 85, no. 3 (2009): 618–619, https://doi.org/10.1353/lan.0.0132.

23. "Languages," UNESCO World Atlas of Languages, accessed May 3, 2023, https://en.wal.unesco.org/discover/languages.

24. Campbell and Belew, *Cataloguing the World's Endangered Languages*.

25. Nala H. Lee and John R. Van Way, "The Language Endangerment Index," in *Cataloguing the World's Endangered Languages*, ed. Lyle Campbell and Anna Belew (London: Routledge, 2018), 66–78, https://doi.org/10.4324/9781315 686028-5.

26. Lenore A. Grenoble, "A Response to 'Assessing Levels of Endangerment in the Catalogue of Endangered Languages (ELCat) Using the Language Endangerment Index (LEI),' by Nala Huiying Lee & John Van Way," *Language in Society* 45, no. 2 (2016): 293–300.

## Chapter 2

1. Harald Hammarström et al., *Glottolog 4.7* (Leipzig: Max Planck Institute for Evolutionary Biology, 2022), https://doi.org/10.5281/zenodo.7398962.

2. Elizabeth Kolbert, "Civilization and Extinction," in *The Climate Book*, by Greta Thunberg (London: Allen Lane, 2022), 11–17.

3. Ezequiel Koile et al., "Phylogeographic Analysis of the Bantu Language Expansion Supports a Rainforest Route," *Proceedings of the National Academy of Sciences of the United States of America* 119, no. 32 (2022): 2112853119, https://doi.org/10.1073/pnas.2112853119.

4. Brigitte Pakendorf and Mark Stoneking, "The Genomic Prehistory of Peoples Speaking Khoisan Languages," *Human Molecular Genetics* 30, no. R1 (2021): 49–55, https://doi.org/10.1093/hmg/ddaa221.

5. Zygmunt Frajzyngier and Erin Shay, "Contact and Afroasiatic Languages," in *The Handbook of Language Contact*, ed. Raymond Hickey (Hoboken, NJ: Wiley-Blackwell, 2020), 571–591, https://doi.org/10.1002/9781119485094.ch29.

6. Hammarström et al., *Glottolog 4.7*.

7. Kolbert, "Civilization and Extinction"; "When Did Modern Humans Get to Australia?," Australian Museum, accessed May 4, 2023, https://australian .museum/learn/science/human-evolution/the-spread-of-people-to-australia /australian.museum/learn/science/human-evolution/the-spread-of-people-to -australia/.

8. Iosif Lazaridis et al., "The Genetic History of the Southern Arc: A Bridge between West Asia and Europe," *Science* 377, no. 6609 (2022): eabm4247, https://doi.org/10.1126/science.abm4247.

9. Remco Bouckaert et al., "Mapping the Origins and Expansion of the Indo-European Language Family," *Science* 337, no. 6097 (2012): 957–960, https:// doi.org/10.1126/science.1219669.

10. Laurent Sagart et al., "Dated Language Phylogenies Shed Light on the Ancestry of Sino-Tibetan," *Proceedings of the National Academy of Sciences of the United States of America* 116, no. 21 (2019): 10317–10322, https://doi.org/10.1073/pnas.1817972116.

11. Vishnupriya Kolipakam et al., "A Bayesian Phylogenetic Study of the Dravidian Language Family," *Royal Society Open Science* 5, no. 3 (2018): 171504, https://doi.org/10.1098/rsos.171504.

12. Martine Robbeets et al., "Triangulation Supports Agricultural Spread of the Transeurasian Languages," *Nature* 599 (2021): 616–621, doi:10.1038/s41586-021-04108-8.

13. For a recent controversy, see Zheng Tian et al., "Triangulation Fails When Neither Linguistic, Genetic, nor Archaeological Data Support the Transeurasian Narrative," 2022, https://doi.org/10.1101/2022.06.09.495471.

14. Johanna Nichols, "The Origin and Dispersal of Uralic: Distributional Typological View," *Annual Review of Linguistics* 7, no. 1 (2021): 351–369, https://doi.org/10.1146/annurev-linguistics-011619-030405.

15. Hammarström et al., *Glottolog* 4.7.

16. Kolbert, "Civilization and Extinction."

17. Michael C. Gavin et al., "Process-Based Modelling Shows How Climate and Demography Shape Language Diversity," *Global Ecology and Biogeography: A Journal of Macroecology* 26, no. 5 (2017): 584–591, https://doi.org/10.1111/geb.12563.

18. Claire Bowern, "How Many Languages Are and Were in Australia?," in *The Oxford Guide to Australian Languages*, ed. Claire Bowern (Oxford: Oxford University Press, 2023), 56–64.

19. Hammarström et al., *Glottolog* 4.7.

20. Russel D. Gray, Alexei J. Drummond, and Simon J. Greenhill, "Language Phylogenies Reveal Expansion Pulses and Pauses in Pacific Settlement," *Science* 323, no. 5913 (2009): 479–483, https://doi.org/10.1126/science.1166858.

21. Hammarström et al., *Glottolog* 4.7.

22. Kolbert, "Civilization and Extinction."

23. Bill Chappell, "The Vatican Repudiates 'Doctrine of Discovery,' Which Was Used to Justify Colonialism," NPR, March 30, 2023, sec. Religion, https://www.npr.org/2023/03/30/1167056438/vatican-doctrine-of-discovery-colonialism-indigenous.

24. Hammarström et al., *Glottolog* 4.7.

25. Johanna Nichols, "Modeling Ancient Population Structures and Movement in Linguistics," *Annual Review of Anthropology* 26 (1997): 359–384.

26. Simon J. Greenhill et al., "A Recent Northern Origin for the Uto-Aztecan Family," *Language* 99, no. 1 (March 2023): 81–107, https://doi.org/10.1353/lan.2023.0006.

27. Hammarström et al., *Glottolog* 4.7.

28. Melanie McKay-Cody, "Memory Comes before Knowledge—North American Indigenous Deaf: Socio-Cultural Study of Rock/Picture Writing, Community, Sign Languages, and Kinship" (PhD diss., University of Oklahoma, 2019), https://shareok.org/handle/11244/319767.

29. Rik Van Gijn et al., "The Social Lives of Isolates (and Small Language Families): The Case of the Northwest Amazon," *Interface Focus* 13, no. 1 (February 6, 2023): 20220054, https://doi.org/10.1098/rsfs.2022.0054.

30. "Povos Isolados," Fundação Nacional dos Povos Indígenas, accessed January 31, 2023, https://www.gov.br/funai/pt-br/atuacao/povos-indigenas/povos-indigenas-isolados-e-de-recente-contato-2/povos-isolados-1.

31. Van Gijn et al., "The Social Lives of Isolates (and Small Language Families)."

32. Van Gijn et al., "The Social Lives of Isolates (and Small Language Families)."

33. Van Gijn et al., "The Social Lives of Isolates (and Small Language Families)."

34. Van Gijn et al., "The Social Lives of Isolates (and Small Language Families)."

35. Hammarström et al., *Glottolog* 4.7.

**Chapter 3**

1. Charles Darwin, *The Descent of Man, and Selection in Relation to Sex* (London: John Murray, 1871), 59–60.

2. Oksana Yakushko, "Eugenics and Its Evolution in the History of Western Psychology: A Critical Archival Review," *Psychotherapy and Politics International* 17, no. 2 (June 2019), https://doi.org/10.1002/ppi.1495.

3. American Psychological Association, "Apology to People of Color for APA's Role in Promoting, Perpetuating, and Failing to Challenge Racism, Racial Discrimination, and Human Hierarchy in U.S." (Washington, DC: American Psychological Association, 2021), https://www.apa.org/about/policy/racism-apology.

4. American Society of Human Genetics, "Facing Our History—Building an Equitable Future," 2023, 3, https://www.ashg.org/wp-content/uploads/2023/01/Executive-Summary_Facing-Our-History-Buildinh-an-Equitable-Future-012023.pdf.

5. David Harmon and Jonathan Loh, "Congruence between Species and Language Diversity," in *The Oxford Handbook of Endangered Languages*, ed. Kenneth L. Rehg and Lyle Campbell (Oxford: Oxford University Press, 2018), 658–682, https://doi.org/10.1093/oxfordhb/9780190610029.013.31.

6. "IUCN Red List of Threatened Species," Resource, IUCN, accessed February 12, 2023, https://www.iucn.org/resources/conservation-tool/iucn-red-list -threatened-species.

7. Michael Krauss, "The World's Languages in Crisis," *Language* 68, no. 1 (1992): 4–10, https://doi.org/10.1353/lan.1992.0075.

8. Jason W. Moore, *Capitalism in the Web of Life: Ecology and the Accumulation of Capital* (New York: Verso Books, 2015).

9. Ruth Mace and Mark Pagel, "A Latitudinal Gradient in the Density of Human Languages in North America," in *Proceedings of the Royal Society B: Biological Sciences* 261, no 1360 (1995): 117–121, https://doi.org/10.1098 /rspb.1995.0125.

10. Jacob Bock Axelsen and Susanna Manrubia, "River Density and Landscape Roughness Are Universal Determinants of Linguistic Diversity," *Proceedings of the Royal Society B: Biological Sciences* 281, no. 1784 (June 7, 2014): 20133029, https://doi.org/10.1098/rspb.2013.3029.

11. Marco Túlio Pacheco Coelho et al., "Drivers of Geographical Patterns of North American Language Diversity," in *Proceedings of the Royal Society B: Biological Sciences* 286 (2019): 20190242, https://doi.org/10.1098/rspb .2019.0242.

12. Pacheco Coelho et al., "Drivers of Geographical Patterns of North American Language Diversity."

13. Walter Mignolo, *The Politics of Decolonial Investigations* (Durham, NC: Duke University Press, 2021).

14. Gurminder K. Bhambra, "A Decolonial Project for Europe," *JCMS: Journal of Common Market Studies* 60, no. 2 (March 2022): 229–244, https://doi .org/10.1111/jcms.13310.

15. Polly Rizova and John Stone, "Race, Ethnicity, and Nation," in *Oxford Research Encyclopedia of International Studies*, ed. Polly Rizova and John Stone (Oxford: Oxford University Press, 2010), https://doi.org/10.1093 /acrefore/9780190846626.013.470.

16. Nelly Bekus, "Reassembling Society in a Nation-State: History, Language, and Identity Discourses of Belarus," *Nationalities Papers* (July 1, 2022): 1–16, https://doi.org/10.1017/nps.2022.60.

17. Benedict Anderson, *Imagined Communities: Reflections on the Origin and Spread of Nationalism* (London: Verso, 1983).

18. Harold F. Schiffman, *Linguistic Culture and Language Policy* (London: Routledge, 1996), 97.

19. Quoted in Schiffman, *Linguistic Culture and Language Policy*, 102.

20. Salikoko S. Mufwene, *The Ecology of Language Evolution* (Cambridge: Cambridge University Press, 2001), https://doi.org/10.1017/cbo9780511612862.

21. Ngũgĩ wa Thiong'o, *Decolonizing the Mind: The Politics of Language in African Literature* (London: J. Currey, 1986), 28.

22. Roxanne Dunbar-Ortiz, *An Indigenous Peoples' History of the United States* (Boston: Beacon Press, 2014); Linda Tuhiwai Smith, "Not Our Apocalypse," Knowledge in Indigenous Networks, April 7, 2020, https://indigenousknow ledgenetwork.net/webinar-2020/.

23. Noble David Cook, *Born to Die: Disease and New World Conquest, 1492–1650* (Cambridge: Cambridge University Press, 1998); Smith, "Not Our Apocalypse."

24. Michael Hironymous, "Santa María Ixcatlan, Oaxaca: From Colonial Cacicazgo to Modern Municipio" (PhD diss., University of Texas at Austin, 2007), http://hdl.handle.net/2152/13258.

25. Truth and Reconciliation Commission of Canada, "Honouring the Truth, Reconciling for the Future: Summary of the Final Report of the Truth and Reconciliation Commission of Canada," 2015, https://archive.org/details/honour ingtruthre0000trut; Bryan Newland, "Federal Indian Boarding School Initiative Investigative Report," May 2022, https://www.bia.gov/sites/default/files /dup/inline-files/bsi_investigative_report_may_2022_508.pdf.

26. "Pope Lands in Canada, Apologizing for the Church's Indigenous Abuse," NBC News, accessed January 31, 2023, https://www.nbcnews.com/nightly -news/video/pope-lands-in-canada-apologizing-for-the-church-s-indigenous -abuse-144693317753.

27. Rauna Kuokkanen, "Reconciliation as a Threat or Structural Change? The Truth and Reconciliation Process and Settler Colonial Policy Making in Finland," *Human Rights Review* 21, no. 3 (September 2020): 293–312, https://doi .org/10.1007/s12142-020-00594-x.

28. Alexis Tiouka and Hélène Ferrarini, *Petit guerrier pour la paix: Les luttes amérindiennes racontées à la jeunesse (et à tous les curieux)* (Matoury, Guyane: Ibis Rouge, 2017).

29. Ngũgĩ, *Decolonizing the Mind*, 11.

30. Quoted in Te Kāhui Tika Tangata / New Zealand Human Rights Commission, *Maranga Mai!* (Wellington: New Zealand Human Rights Commission, November 2022), https://admin.tikatangata.org.nz/assets/Documents /Maranga-Mai_Full-Report_PDF.pdf.

31. Te Kāhui Tika Tangata / New Zealand Human Rights Commission, *Maranga Mai!*

32. Gerald Roche, "Linguistic Injustice, Decolonization, and Language Endangerment," EasyChair Preprint no. 1726, 2019, https://easychair.org/publications/preprint/JsQp.

33. "Catálogo de las lenguas indígenas nacionales," accessed May 3, 2023, https://www.inali.gob.mx/clin-inali/#agrupaciones.

34. Yásnaya Elena Aguilar Gil, *Ää: Manifiestos sobre la diversidad lingüística* (Mexico City: Almadía, 2020).

35. Donald F. Moores, "Partners in Progress: The 21st International Congress on Education of the Deaf and the Repudiation of the 1880 Congress of Milan," *American Annals of the Deaf* 155, no. 3 (2010): 309–310, https://doi.org/10.1353/aad.2010.0016.

36. Corinne Chin, "The Fight to Save Hawaii Sign Language from Extinction," CNN, accessed February 14, 2023, https://www.cnn.com/2021/10/08/americas/hawaii-sign-language-extinction-as-equals-intl-cmd/index.html.

37. Dave Eggers, *What Is the What: The Autobiography of Valentino Achak Deng* (San Francisco: McSweeney's, 2006).

38. Ahmed A. Beriar and Hussein Abdo Rababah, "The Endangerment of the Nubiin Language: Sociolinguistics, Language Policy and Literacy Perspectives," *International Journal of Applied Linguistics and Translation* 2, no. 1 (2016): 1–7, https://doi.org/10.11648/j.ijalt.20160201.11.

39. Sinfree Makoni, Cristine Severo, and Ashraf Abdelhay, "Postcolonial Language Policy and Planning and the Limits of the Notion of the Modern State," *Annual Review of Linguistics* 9, no. 1 (January 17, 2023): 483–496, https://doi.org/10.1146/annurev-linguistics-030521-052930; Robert Melson, "Modern Genocide in Rwanda: Ideology, Revolution, War, and Mass Murder in an African State," in *The Specter of Genocide*, ed. Robert Gellately and Ben Kiernan (Cambridge: Cambridge University Press, 2003), 325–338, https://doi.org/10.1017/CBO9780511819674.015.

40. Sarah Bunin Benor and Bernard Spolsky, "Changes in the Sociolinguistic Ecology of Jewish Communities," in *Handbook of the Changing World Language Map*, ed. Stanley D. Brunn and Roland Kehrein (Cham: Springer International Publishing, 2020), 1027–1036, https://doi.org/10.1007/978-3-030-02438-3_9.

41. Cook, *Born to Die*.

42. José Francisco Cali Tzay, "'COVID-19 Is Devastating Indigenous Communities Worldwide, and It's Not Only about Health'—UN Expert Warns," United Nations Human Rights Office of the High Commissioner, May 18, 2020, https://www.ohchr.org/en/press-releases/2020/05/covid-19-devastating-indigenous-communities-worldwide-and-its-not-only-about.

43. Smith, "Not Our Apocalypse."

44. Jill Langlois, "Losing Elders to COVID-19 Endangers Indigenous Languages," *National Geographic*, November 13, 2020, https://www.nationalgeo graphic.com/history/article/losing-elders-to-covid-19-endangers-indigenous -languages.

45. Onowa McIvor, Kari A. B. Chew, and Kahtehrón:ni Iris Stacey, "Indigenous Language Learning Impacts, Challenges and Opportunities in COVID-19 Times," *AlterNative: An International Journal of Indigenous Peoples* 16, no. 4 (December 2020): 409–412, https://doi.org/10.1177/1177180120970930.

46. IPCC, *Global Warming of 1.5°C: IPCC Special Report on Impacts of Global Warming of 1.5°C above Pre-Industrial Levels in Context of Strengthening Response to Climate Change, Sustainable Development, and Efforts to Eradicate Poverty* (Cambridge: Cambridge University Press, 2022), https://doi.org/10 .1017/9781009157940.

## Chapter 4

1. "United Nations Declaration on the Rights of Indigenous Peoples | United Nations for Indigenous Peoples," accessed January 31, 2023, https://www .un.org/development/desa/indigenouspeoples/declaration-on-the-rights-of -indigenous-peoples.html.

2. United Nations, "United Nations Convention on the Rights of the Child," 1990, https://www.ohchr.org/en/instruments-mechanisms/instruments/con vention-rights-child.

3. Tove Skutnabb-Kangas and Robert Phillipson, "Linguicide and Linguicism," in *Contact Linguistics: An International Handbook of Contemporary Research*, ed. Hans Goebl, Peter H. Nelde, Zdenek Stary, and Wolfgang Wölck (Berlin: De Gruyter, 1996), 1:667–675, https://doi.org/10.1515/9783110132649.1.6 .667.

4. Roxanne Dunbar-Ortiz, *An Indigenous Peoples' History of the United States* (Boston: Beacon Press, 2014).

5. Papaarangi Reid, Donna Cormack, and Sarah-Jane Paine, "Colonial Histories, Racism and Health—the Experience of Māori and Indigenous Peoples," *Public Health* 172 (July 2019): 119–124, https://doi.org/10.1016/j.puhe .2019.03.027.

6. Hugh Brody, "'The Deepest Silences': What Lies behind the Arctic's Indigenous Suicide Crisis," *Guardian*, July 21, 2022, https://www.theguardian.com /news/2022/jul/21/the-deepest-silences-what-lies-behind-the-indigenous -suicide-crisis.

7. Mary P. Koss et al., "Adverse Childhood Exposures and Alcohol Dependence among Seven Native American Tribes," *American Journal of Preventive Medicine* 25, no. 3 (2003): 238–244, https://doi.org/10.1016/s0749-3797(03)00195-8.

8. "Aboriginal Community Controlled Health—NACCHO," accessed January 31, 2023, https://www.naccho.org.au/acchos/.

9. D. H. Whalen et al., "Health Effects of Indigenous Language Use and Revitalization: A Realist Review," *International Journal for Equity in Health* 21, no. 1 (November 28, 2022): 169, https://doi.org/10.1186/s12939-022-01782-6.

10. Darcy Hallett, Michael J. Chandler, and Christopher E. Lalonde, "Aboriginal Language Knowledge and Youth Suicide," *Cognitive Development* 22, no. 3 (2007): 392–399, https://doi.org/10.1016/j.cogdev.2007.02.001.

11. Les B. Whitbeck et al., "Perceived Discrimination and Early Substance Abuse among American Indian Children," *Journal of Health and Social Behavior* 42, no. 4 (December 2001): 405–424, https://doi.org/10.2307/3090187.

12. Richard T. Oster et al., "Cultural Continuity, Traditional Indigenous Language, and Diabetes in Alberta First Nations: A Mixed Methods Study," *International Journal for Equity in Health* 13 (October 2014): 92, https://doi.org/10.1186/s12939-014-0092-4.

13. Yontan Dinku et al., "Language Use Is Connected to Indicators of Wellbeing: Evidence from the National Aboriginal and Torres Strait Islander Social Survey 2014/15," Australian National University, 2020, https://doi.org/10.25911/5DDB9FD6394E8.

14. Karina L. Walters et al., "Growing from Our Roots: Strategies for Developing Culturally Grounded Health Promotion Interventions in American Indian, Alaska Native, and Native Hawaiian Communities," *Prevention Science* 21, no. S1 (January 2020): 54–64, https://doi.org/10.1007/s11121-018-0952-z.

15. Arjun Appadurai, *Modernity at Large: Cultural Dimensions of Globalization* (Minneapolis: University of Minnesota Press, 1996), https://play.google.com/store/books/details?id=4LVeJT7gghMC.

16. "Kinship Module," University of Sydney, accessed September 16, 2023, https://www.sydney.edu.au/about-us/vision-and-values/our-aboriginal-and-torres-strait-islander-community/kinship-module.html.

17. Nicholas Evans, "Context, Culture, and Structuration in the Languages of Australia," *Annual Review of Anthropology* 32 (2003): 13–40.

18. Rodrigo Cámara-Leret and Jordi Bascompte, "Language Extinction Triggers the Loss of Unique Medicinal Knowledge," *Proceedings of the National Academy of Sciences of the United States of America* 118, no 24 (2021): e2103683118, https://doi.org/10.1073/pnas.2103683118.

19. Susan Chiblow and Paul J. Meighan, "Language Is Land, Land Is Language: The Importance of Indigenous Languages," *Human Geography* 15, no. 2 (2022): 206–210, https://doi.org/10.1177/19427786211022899.

20. Selene Rangel-Landa et al., "Ixcatec Ethnoecology: Plant Management and Biocultural Heritage in Oaxaca, Mexico," *Journal of Ethnobiology and Ethnomedicine* 12 (2016): 30, https://doi.org/10.1186/s13002-016-0101-3.

21. Leanne Betasamosake Simpson, *Dancing on Our Turtle's Back* (Winnipeg: Arbeiter Ring Publishing, 2011).

22. Damián E. Blasi et al., "Over-Reliance on English Hinders Cognitive Science," *Trends in Cognitive Sciences* 26, no. 12 (2022): 1153–1170, https://doi.org/10.1016/j.tics.2022.09.015.

23. Edward Gibson et al., "Color Naming across Languages Reflects Color Use," *Proceedings of the National Academy of Sciences of the United States of America* 114, no. 40 (2017): 10785–10790, https://doi.org/10.1073/pnas.1619666114.

24. Peggy Li and Lila Gleitman, "Turning the Tables: Language and Spatial Reasoning," *Cognition* 83, no. 3 (April 2002): 265–294, https://doi.org/10.1016/S0010-0277(02)00009-4.

25. Rafael E. Núñez and Eve Sweetser, "With the Future behind Them: Convergent Evidence from Aymara Language and Gesture in the Crosslinguistic Comparison of Spatial Construals of Time," *Cognitive Science* 30, no. 3 (2006): 401–450, https://doi.org/10.1207/s15516709cog0000_62.

26. Lera Boroditsky and Alice Gaby, "Remembrances of Times East: Absolute Spatial Representations of Time in an Australian Aboriginal Community," *Psychological Science* 21, no. 11 (2010): 1635–1639, https://doi.org/10.1177/0956797610386621.

27. Rafael Núñez, Kensy Cooperrider, D. Doan, and Jürg Wassmann, "Contours of Time: Topographic Construals of Past, Present, and Future in the Yupno Valley of Papua New Guinea," *Cognition* 124, no. 1 (2012): 25–35, https://doi.org/10.1016/j.cognition.2012.03.007.

28. Blasi et al., "Over-Reliance on English Hinders Cognitive Science."

29. Evangelia Adamou and Yair Haendler, "An Experimental Approach to Nominal Tense: Evidence from Pomak (Slavic)," *Language* 96, no. 3 (2020): 507–550, https://doi.org/10.1353/lan.2020.0040.

30. Nan B. Ratner and Clifton Pye, "Higher Pitch in BT Is Not Universal: Acoustic Evidence from Quiche Mayan," *Journal of Child Language* 11, no. 3 (1984): 515–522, https://doi.org/10.1017/s0305000900005924.

31. Marisa Casillas, Penelope Brown, and Stephen C. Levinson, "Early Language Experience in a Papuan Community," *Journal of Child Language* 48, no. 4 (2021): 792–814, https://doi.org/10.1017/S0305000920000549; Georgia

Loukatou et al., "Child-Directed and Overheard Input from Different Speakers in Two Distinct Cultures," *Journal of Child Language* 49, no. 6 (2022): 1173–1192, https://doi.org/10.1017/S0305000921000623.

32. Rachid Ridouane, "Syllables without Vowels: Phonetic and Phonological Evidence from Tashlhiyt Berber," *Phonology* 25, no. 2 (2008): 321–359.

33. Hedvig Skirgård et al., "Grambank Reveals the Importance of Genealogical Constraints on Linguistic Diversity and Highlights the Impact of Language Loss," *Science Advances* 9, no. 16 (April 2023): eadg6175, https://doi.org/10.1126/sciadv.adg6175.

### Chapter 5

1. "Wôpanâak Language Reclamation Project," WLRP, accessed May 3, 2023, https://www.wlrp.org.

2. Jessie Little Doe Fermino, "An Introduction to Wampanoag Grammar" (master's thesis, Massachusetts Institute of Technology, 2000), https://dspace.mit.edu/handle/1721.1/8740.

3. Wesley Y. Leonard, "Producing Language Reclamation by Decolonising 'Language,'" *Language Documentation and Description* 14 (2017): 15–36, https://doi.org/10.25894/ldd146.

4. "Council Recommendation of 12 March 2021 on Roma Equality, Inclusion and Participation 2021/C 93/01," EUR-Lex, 2021, https://eur-lex.europa.eu/legal-content/EN/TXT/?uri=CELEX:32021H0319(01).

5. Pius W. Akumbu, "Language Documentation and the Empowerment of Target Community Members | SOAS University of London," YouTube, 2021, https://www.youtube.com/watch?v=IEb5yCf0TOA.

6. Winona LaDuke, *All Our Relations: Native Struggles for Land and Life* (Chicago: Haymarket Books, 2015).

7. Leketi Makalela, "Community Elders' Narrative Accounts of Ubuntu Translanguaging: Learning and Teaching in African Education," *International Review of Education* 64, no. 6 (December 2018): 838, https://doi.org/10.1007/s11159-018-9752-8.

8. Gabriela Pérez Báez, Rachel Vogel, and Uia Patolo, "Global Survey of Revitalization Efforts: A Mixed Methods Approach to Understanding Language Revitalization Practices," *Language Documentation and Conservation* 13 (2019): 446–513, https://scholarspace.manoa.hawaii.edu/handle/10125/24871.

9. Janne Underriner et al., "Teaching Strategies for Language Revitalization and Maintenance," in *Revitalizing Endangered Languages*, ed. Justyna Olko and Julia Sallabank (Cambridge: Cambridge University Press, 2021), 235–272, https://doi.org/10.1017/9781108641142.016.

10. Underriner et al., "Teaching Strategies for Language Revitalization and Maintenance."

11. "American Indian Language Development Institute," University of Arizona, accessed September 17, 2023, https://aildi.arizona.edu/; "Canadian Indigenous Languages and Literacy Development Institute," University of Alberta, accessed May 2, 2023, https://www.ualberta.ca/canadian-indigenous-languages-and-literacy-development-institute/index.html; "Institute on Collaborative Language Research," CoLang, accessed September 17, 2023, https://www.colanginstitute.org; "Northwest Indian Language Institute," NILI, accessed May 2, 2023, https://nili.uoregon.edu/.

12. Michael Shaub, "Wearable SkoBots Full of Steam and Vanishing Indigenous Languages," Hackaday, 2023, https://hackaday.com/2023/01/03/wearable-skobots-full-of-steam-and-vanishing-indigenous-languages/.

13. "Learn Anishinaabemowin," Anishinaabemdaa, accessed January 31, 2023, https://anishinaabemdaa.com/.

14. Genner Llanes Ortiz, "Art, Music and Cultural Activities," in *Revitalizing Endangered Languages*, ed. Justyna Olko and Julia Sallabank (Cambridge: Cambridge University Press, 2021), 273–296, https://doi.org/10.1017/978110 8641142.017.

15. Jennifer Green, Inge Kral, and Sally Treloyn, "The Verbal Arts in Indigenous Australia," in *The Oxford Guide to Australian Languages*, ed. Claire Bowern (Oxford: Oxford University Press, 2023), 591–600.

16. "West Australian Opera—Koolbardi Wer Wardong," West Australian Opera, accessed January 31, 2023, https://www.waopera.asn.au/shows/past-seasons/season-2021/koolbardi-wer-wardong/; Sadie Brink, "Otyken—Giving Voice to East Siberian Indigenous Culture," PopKult, June 13, 2022, https://popkult.org/otyken-khakas-chulym-indigenous/.

17. Harold F. Schiffman, *Linguistic Culture and Language Policy* (Hoboken, NJ: Taylor and Francis, 2012).

18. Nancy Hornberger, "Frameworks and Models in Language Policy and Planning," in *An Introduction to Language Policy: Theory and Method*, ed. Thomas Ricento (Malden, MA: Blackwell, 2006), 24–41.

19. South African Department of Arts and Culture, "National Language Policy Framework," 2003, http://www.dac.gov.za/sites/default/files/LPD_Language%20Policy%20Framework_English_0.pdf.

20. Hornberger, "Frameworks and Models in Language Policy and Planning."

21. South African Department of Arts and Culture, "National Language Policy Framework."

22. Departament de la Presidencia, "DECRET 106/1982, de 16 d'abril, Sobre Senyalització de Carreteres, Estacions Ferroviàries, d'autobusos i Serveis Públics En l'àmbit Territorial de La Comunitat Autònoma," Pub. L. No. DE-CRET 106/1982 (1982), https://vlex.es/vid/senyalitzacio-ries-autobusos-mbit -noma-38338155.

23. "The Inuit Heritage Trust (IHT)," accessed January 31, 2023, http://www .ihti.ca/eng/projectsn.html.

24. "The Inuit Heritage Trust (IHT)."

25. Hornberger, "Frameworks and Models in Language Policy and Planning."

26. Gerald Roche, "Articulating Language Oppression: Colonialism, Colo-niality and the Erasure of Tibet's Minority Languages," *Patterns of Prejudice* 53, no. 5 (October 20, 2019): 487–514, https://doi.org/10.1080/0031322X .2019.1662074.

27. Cecilia Macaulay, "Nigerian Schools: Flogged for Speaking My Mother Tongue," BBC News, January 7, 2023, https://www.bbc.com/news/world-africa -63971991.

28. Government of India, "National Education Policy 2020," 2020, https:// www.education.gov.in/sites/upload_files/mhrd/files/NEP_Final_English_0.pdf.

29. Rupanjali Karthik and George W. Noblit, "Language Policy and Reform in the Indian School System," in *Oxford Research Encyclopedia of Education*, ed. Ru-panjali Karthik and George W. Noblit (Oxford: Oxford University Press, 2020), https://doi.org/10.1093/acrefore/9780190264093.013.836.

30. Bernard Spolsky, *Language Policy* (Cambridge: Cambridge University Press, 2004).

31. Monica Heller, "Language and the Nation-State: Challenges to Sociolin-guistic Theory and Practice," *Journal of Sociolinguistics* 12, no. 4 (September 2008): 511, https://doi.org/10.1111/j.1467-9841.2008.00373.x.

32. Esteban Acuña Cabanzo, Evangelia Adamou, and Cristian Padure, "On-line Survey on Romani Dispositions towards Language Policy in Colombia and Romania" (unpublished manuscript, 2020); Cristian Padure and Evangelia Ad-amou, "The Activity Spheres Framework Applied to Language Policy: Disposi-tions towards Romani Revitalization in Romania" (preprint, submitted June 23, 2021), halshs-03268416.

33. "Nau mai," Te Taura Whiri I Te Reo Māori, accessed January 31, 2023, https://en.tetaurawhiri.govt.nz/.

34. "Nau mai."

35. "About the European Charter for Regional or Minority Languages," Coun-cil of Europe Portal, accessed January 31, 2023, https://www.coe.int/en/web /european-charter-regional-or-minority-languages/about-the-charter.

36. "Indigenous Languages," UN Permanent Forum on Indigenous Issues, 2018, https://www.un.org/development/desa/indigenouspeoples/wp-content/uploads/sites/19/2018/04/Indigenous-Languages.pdf.

37. "Global Action Plan of the International Decade of Indigenous Languages (2022–2032)," UNESCO Digital Library, accessed January 31, 2023, https://unesdoc.unesco.org/ark:/48223/pf0000379853.

## Chapter 6

1. Emma Webster et al., "The Killer Boomerang and Other Lessons Learnt on the Journey to Undertaking Community-Led Research," in *Community-Led Research*, ed. Victoria Rawlings, James L. Flexner, and Lynette Riley (Sydney: Sydney University Press, 2021), 73–88, http://www.jstor.org/stable/j.ctv1rcf2jj.7.

2. Wesley Y. Leonard and Erin Haynes, "Making 'Collaboration' Collaborative: An Examination of Perspectives That Frame Linguistic Field Research," *Language Documentation and Conservation* 4 (2010): 269–293, http://hdl.handle.net/10125/4482.

3. "Principles of Professional Responsibility," AAA Ethics Forum, accessed January 31, 2023, https://ethics.americananthro.org/ethics-statement-0-preamble/.

4. Himani Bhakuni and Seye Abimbola, "Epistemic Injustice in Academic Global Health," *Lancet Global Health* 9, no. 10 (October 2021): e1465–e1470, https://doi.org/10.1016/S2214-109X(21)00301-6.

5. Joanne Rappaport, *Cowards Don't Make History: Orlando Fals Borda and the Origins of Participatory Action Research* (Durham, NC: Duke University Press, 2020), https://doi.org/10.2307/j.ctv16qjzcx.

6. Linda Tuhiwai Smith, *Decolonizing Methodologies: Research and Indigenous Peoples*, 2nd ed. (London: Zed Books, 2012).

7. Margaret Kovach, *Indigenous Methodologies: Characteristics, Conversations, and Contexts*, 2nd ed. (Toronto: University of Toronto Press, 2021).

8. Wendy Makoons Geniusz, *Our Knowledge Is Not Primitive: Decolonizing Botanical Anishinaabe Teachings* (Syracuse, NY: Syracuse University Press, 2009), 9–10.

9. Dawn Bessarab and Bridget Ng'andu, "Yarning about Yarning as a Legitimate Method in Indigenous Research," *International Journal of Cooperative Information Systems* 3 (2010): 37–50.

10. In Aotearoa New Zealand, only 5 percent of the academic staff is Māori. Jacinta Ruru and Linda Waimarie Nikora, eds., *Ngā Kete Mātauranga: Māori*

*Scholars at the Research Interface* (Dunedin, New Zealand: Otago University Press, Te Whare Tā o Te Wānanga o Ōtākou, 2021).

11. "CASC Science Featured in White House Indigenous Knowledge Guidance Report," US Geological Survey," accessed January 31, 2023, https://www.usgs.gov/programs/climate-adaptation-science-centers/news/casc-science-featured-white-house-indigenous.

12. For a critical approach to the use of the term *last speaker*, see Jenny L. Davis, "Famous Last Speakers: Celebrity and Erasure in Media Coverage of Language Endangerment," in *Indigenous Celebrity: Entanglements with Fame*, ed. Jennifer Adese and Robert Alexander Innes (Winnipeg: University of Manitoba Press, 2021), 163–176.

13. Evangelia Adamou, *The Adaptive Bilingual Mind: Insights from Endangered Languages* (Cambridge: Cambridge University Press, 2021).

14. Eréndira Calderón, Stefano De Pascale, and Evangelia Adamou, "How to Speak 'Geocentric' in an 'Egocentric' Language: A Multimodal Study among Ngigua-Spanish Bilinguals and Spanish Monolinguals in a Rural Community of Mexico," *Language Sciences* 74 (July 2019): 24–46, https://doi.org/10.1016/j.langsci.2019.04.001.

15. Evangelia Adamou and Xingjia Rachel Shen, "Beyond Language Shift: Spatial Cognition among the Ixcatecs in Mexico," *Journal of Cognition and Culture* 17, nos. 1–2 (February 8, 2017): 94–115, https://doi.org/10.1163/15685373-12342193.

16. Maïa Ponsonnet, *Difference and Repetition in Language Shift to a Creole: The Expression of Emotions* (London: Routledge, 2021).

17. Hayley Marama Cavino, "He Would Not Listen to a Woman: Decolonizing Gender through the Power of Pūrākau," in *Decolonizing Research: Indigenous Storywork as Methodology*, ed. Jo-Ann Archibald et al. (London: Zed Books, 2019), 95–106.

18. Rosa Vallejos, *A Grammar of Kukama-Kukamiria: A Language from the Amazon* (Leiden: Brill, 2016).

19. Jonathan Harrington and Ulrich Reubold, "Accent Reversion in Older Adults: Evidence from the Queen's Christmas Broadcasts," in *Language Variation and Language Change across the Lifespan*, ed. Karen V. Beaman and Isabelle Buchstaller (New York: Routledge, 2021), 119–137.

20. Barbara Köpke and Monika S. Schmid, "Language Attrition: The Next Phase," in *First Language Attrition: Interdisciplinary Perspectives on Methodological Issues*, ed. Monika S. Schmid et al. (Amsterdam: John Benjamins Publishing Company, 2004), 1, https://doi.org/10.1075/sibil.28.02kop.

21. Monika S. Schmid and Merel Keijzer, "First Language Attrition and Reversion among Older Migrants," *International Journal of the Sociology of Language* 200 (2009): 83–101, https://doi.org/10.1515/IJSL.2009.046.

22. Monika S. Schmid, *First Language Attrition, Use and Maintenance: The Case of German Jews in Anglophone Countries* (Amsterdam: John Benjamins Publishing Company, 2002).

23. "Reclaiming My Language," First Peoples Cultural Council, accessed January 31, 2023, https://fpcc.ca/program/reclaiming-my-language/.

24. Daria Boltokova, "'Will the Real Semi-Speaker Please Stand Up?' Language Vitality, Semi-Speakers, and Problems of Enumeration in the Canadian North," *Anthropologica* 59, no. 1 (2017): 12–27.

25. The exact figures are as follows: 24 percent of all languages are described in a grammar that has more than three hundred pages, 10 percent in a grammar of less than three hundred pages, and 26 percent in a grammar sketch. For further information, see "GlottoScope," Glottolog, accessed September 18, 2023, https://glottolog.org/langdoc/status.

26. Evangelia Adamou, Quentin Feltgen, and Cristian Padure, "A Unified Approach to the Study of Language Contact: Cross-Language Priming and Change in Adjective/Noun Order," *International Journal of Bilingualism* 25, no. 6 (2021): 1635–1654, https://doi.org/10.1177/13670069211033909.

27. Stanislas Dehaene et al., "Illiterate to Literate: Behavioural and Cerebral Changes Induced by Reading Acquisition," *Nature Reviews Neuroscience* 16, no. 4 (April 2015): 234–244, https://doi.org/10.1038/nrn3924.

28. Evangelia Adamou, *A Corpus-Driven Approach to Language Contact: Endangered Languages in a Comparative Perspective* (Berlin: De Gruyter, 2016).

29. Robert J. Hartsuiker and Kristof Strijkers, *Language Production* (London: Routledge, 2023).

30. Evangelia Adamou, "Experimental Methods to Study Cultural Differences in Linguistics," in *The Routledge Handbook of Experimental Linguistics*, ed. Sandrine Zufferey and Pascal Gygax (London: Routledge, 2024), 458–472, https://shs.hal.science/halshs-04120689/file/Adamou_preprint.pdf.

31. Virginie Ann, "Yukon Sisters Create Southern Tutchone Dictionary," CBC News, January 7, 2023, https://www.cbc.ca/news/canada/north/yukon-southern-tutchone-dictionary-1.6706168.

32. "Dictionaries," accessed January 31, 2023, https://ngumpin.org.au/dictionaries/.

33. Patience L. Epps, Anthony K. Webster, and Anthony C. Woodbury, "A Holistic Humanities of Speaking: Franz Boas and the Continuing Centrality of

Texts," *International Journal of American Linguistics* 83, no. 1 (January 2017): 41–78, https://doi.org/10.1086/689547.

34. Cavino, "He Would Not Listen to a Woman."

35. Jo-Ann Archibald et al., eds., *Decolonizing Research: Indigenous Storywork as Methodology* (London: Zed Books, 2019).

36. "First Nation Language Readers," University of Regina Press, accessed January 31, 2023, https://uofrpress.ca/Series/F/First-Nation-Language-Readers.

## Chapter 7

1. "Internet World Users by Language: Top 10 Languages," Internet World Stats, accessed January 31, 2023, https://www.internetworldstats.com/stats7.htm.

2. "Internet World Users by Language."

3. Pratik Joshi et al., "The State and Fate of Linguistic Diversity and Inclusion in the NLP World," in *Proceedings of the 58th Annual Meeting of the Association for Computational Linguistics* (Online: Association for Computational Linguistics, April 20, 2020), 6282–6293, https://doi.org/10.18653/v1/2020.acl-main.560.

4. Felix Mukwiza Ndahinda and Aggée Shyaka Mugabe, "Streaming Hate: Exploring the Harm of Anti-Banyamulenge and Anti-Tutsi Hate Speech on Congolese Social Media," *Journal of Genocide Research* (May 19, 2022): 1–25, https://doi.org/10.1080/14623528.2022.2078578.

5. Sarah Perez, "Google Translate Adds 24 New Languages, Including Its First Indigenous Languages of the Americas," TechCrunch, May 11, 2022, https://tcrn.ch/3ssxHOX.

6. Damián Blasi, Antonios Anastasopoulos, and Graham Neubig, "Systematic Inequalities in Language Technology Performance across the World's Languages," in *Proceedings of the 60th Annual Meeting of the Association for Computational Linguistics (Volume 1: Long Papers)* (Dublin: Association for Computational Linguistics, 2022), 5486–5505, https://doi.org/10.18653/v1/2022.acl-long.376.

7. "Choose Your Language," Mozilla, accessed January 31, 2023, https://www.mozilla.org/en-US/locales/.

8. Jennyfer Lawrence Taylor et al., "Crocodile Language Friend: Tangibles to Foster Children's Language Use," in *Extended Abstracts of the 2020 CHI Conference on Human Factors in Computing Systems* (Honolulu: ACM, 2020), 1–14, https://doi.org/10.1145/3334480.3383031.

9. Roland Kuhn et al., "The Indigenous Languages Technology Project at NRC Canada: An Empowerment-Oriented Approach to Developing Language

Software," in *Proceedings of the 28th International Conference on Computational Linguistics* (Barcelona: International Committee on Computational Linguistics, 2020), 5866–5878, https://doi.org/10.18653/v1/2020.coling-main.516.

10. Kuhn et al., "The Indigenous Languages Technology Project at NRC Canada."

11. See Story Weaver, https://storyweaver.org.in/.

12. Diana Taylor, *The Archive and the Repertoire: Performing Cultural Memory in the Americas* (Durham, NC: Duke University Press, 2003), https://doi.org/10.2307/j.ctv11smz1k.

13. Patrick D. Nunn et al., "Human Observations of Late Quaternary Coastal Change: Examples from Australia, Europe and the Pacific Islands," *Quaternary International* 638–639 (November 2022): 212–224, https://doi.org/10.1016/j.quaint.2022.06.016.

14. Kirsty Rowan, "Mdocumentation: Combining New Technologies and Language Documentation to Promote Multilingualism in Nubian Heritage Language Learners of the Diaspora," in *Rethinking Language Use in Digital Africa*, ed. Leketi Makalela and Goodith White (Bristol, UK: Multilingual Matters, 2021), 73–96, https://doi.org/10.21832/9781800412316-006.

15. "DOBES Archive," Language Archive, accessed January 31, 2023, https://archive.mpi.nl/tla/islandora/object/tla%3A1839_00_0000_0000_0001_305B_C.

16. Endangered Languages Archive, accessed January 31, 2023, https://www.elararchive.org/.

17. "Welcome to the Archive of the Indigenous Languages of Latin America (AILLA)," Archive of the Indigenous Languages of Latin America, accessed January 31, 2023, https://ailla.utexas.org/; "Pacific and Regional Archive for Digital Sources in Endangered Cultures," PARADISEC, accessed September 19, 2023, https://www.paradisec.org.au/.

18. Boyd Michailovsky et al., "Documenting and Researching Endangered Languages: The Pangloss Collection," *Language Documentation and Conservation* 8 (2014): 119–135, http://hdl.handle.net/10125/4621.

19. Lesley Woods, *Something's Gotta Change: Redefining Collaborative Linguistic Research* (Canberra: ANU Press, 2023), https://doi.org/10.22459/sgc.2022.

20. Cori Hayden, *When Nature Goes Public: The Making and Unmaking of Bioprospecting in Mexico* (Princeton, NJ: Princeton University Press, 2003).

21. Stephanie Russo Carroll et al., "The CARE Principles for Indigenous Data Governance," *Data Science Journal* 19 (November 4, 2020): 43, https://doi.org/10.5334/dsj-2020-043.

22. Woods, *Something's Gotta Change*.

23. Donavyn Coffey, "Māori Are Trying to Save Their Language from Big Tech," *Wired UK*, accessed January 31, 2023, https://www.wired.co.uk/article /maori-language-tech.

24. Keoni Mahelona et al., "OpenAI's Whisper Is Another Case Study in Colonisation," Papa Reo, January 24, 2023, https://blog.papareo.nz/whisper -is-another-case-study-in-colonisation/.

25. Robin R. R. Gray, "Rematriation: Ts'msyen Law, Rights of Relationality, and Protocols of Return," *Native American and Indigenous Studies* 9, no. 1 (March 2022): 1–27, https://doi.org/10.1353/nai.2022.0010.

**Chapter 8**

1. Evangelia Adamou and Andrey Sobolev, eds., *Atlas of the Balkan Linguistic Area*, 2023, abla.cnrs.fr.

2. Victor Friedman and Brian Joseph, *The Balkan Languages* (Cambridge: Cambridge University Press, 2024).

3. Leketi Makalela, "Community Elders' Narrative Accounts of Ubuntu Translanguaging: Learning and Teaching in African Education," *International Review of Education* 64, no. 6 (December 2018): 837, https://doi.org/10.1007 /s11159-018-9752-8.

4. Sinfree Makoni, Cristine Severo, and Ashraf Abdelhay, "Postcolonial Language Policy and Planning and the Limits of the Notion of the Modern State," *Annual Review of Linguistics* 9, no. 1 (January 17, 2023): 483–496, https://doi .org/10.1146/annurev-linguistics-030521-052930.

5. A. Barbier, "Sommeil, rêves et expériences visionnaires dans le village koriak de Tymlat (Kamtchatka, Extrême-Orient russe)," *Médecine du Sommeil* 20, no 2 (December 2022): 116–121, https://doi.org/10.1016/j.msom.2022.11.004.

6. Ruth Singer and Salome Harris, "What Practices and Ideologies Support Small-Scale Multilingualism? A Case Study of Warruwi Community, Northern Australia," *International Journal of the Sociology of Language* 2016, no. 241 (January 1, 2016): 163–208, https://doi.org/10.1515/ijsl-2016-0029.

7. US Census Bureau, "Detailed Languages Spoken at Home and Ability to Speak English for the Population 5 Years and Over: 2009–2013," 2022, http:// www.census.gov/data/tables/2013/demo/2009-2013-lang-tables.html; American Councils for International Education, *The National K-12 Foreign Language Enrollment Survey Report* (Washington, DC: American Councils for International Education, 2017), https://www.americancouncils.org/sites/default /files/FLE-report-June17.pdf.

8. Evangelia Adamou, *The Adaptive Bilingual Mind: Insights from Endangered Languages* (Cambridge: Cambridge University Press, 2021).

9. Robert J. Hartsuiker and Kristof Strijkers, *Language Production* (London: Routledge, 2023).

10. Jubin Abutalebi, "Neural Aspects of Second Language Representation and Language Control," *Acta Psychologica* 128, no. 3 (July 2008): 466–478, https://doi.org/10.1016/j.actpsy.2008.03.014.

11. Karen Emmorey et al., "Bimodal Bilingualism," *Bilingualism: Language and Cognition* 11, no. 1 (March 2008): 43–61, https://doi.org/10.1017/S1366728907003203.

12. Shana Poplack, *Borrowing: Loanwords in the Speech Community and in the Grammar* (New York: Oxford University Press, 2018), 36, 54.

13. Evangelia Adamou and Xingjia Rachel Shen, "There Are No Language Switching Costs When Codeswitching Is Frequent," *International Journal of Bilingualism* 23, no. 1 (February 2019): 53–70, https://doi.org/10.1177/1367006917709094.

14. Christos Pliatsikas, "Understanding Structural Plasticity in the Bilingual Brain: The Dynamic Restructuring Model," *Bilingualism: Language and Cognition* 23, no. 2 (2020): 459–471, https://doi.org/10.1017/S1366728919000130.

15. Katherine Woollett and Eleanor A. Maguire, "Acquiring 'the Knowledge' of London's Layout Drives Structural Brain Changes," *Current Biology* 21, no. 24 (December 2011): 2109–2114, https://doi.org/10.1016/j.cub.2011.11.018.

16. D. J. Saer, "The Effect of Bilingualism on Intelligence," *British Journal of Psychology: General Section* 14, no. 1 (July 1923): 38, https://doi.org/10.1111/j.2044-8295.1923.tb00110.x.

17. Elizabeth Peal and Wallace E. Lambert, "The Relation of Bilingualism to Intelligence," *Psychological Monographs: General and Applied* 76, no. 27 (1962): 1–23, https://doi.org/10.1037/h0093840.

18. For an overview of myths and realities about bilingualism, see Krista Byers-Heinlein and Casey Lew-Williams, "Bilingualism in the Early Years: What the Science Says," *LEARNing Landscapes* 7, no. 1 (2013): 95–112.

19. Ellen Bialystok, "Cognitive Implications of Bilingualism," in *Oxford Research Encyclopedia of Psychology*, ed. Oliver Braddick (Oxford: Oxford University Press, 2021), https://doi.org/10.1093/acrefore/9780190236557.013.763.

20. Ofelia García et al., "Rejecting Abyssal Thinking in the Language and Education of Racialized Bilinguals: A Manifesto," *Critical Inquiry in Language Studies* 18, no. 3 (2021): 203–228, https://doi.org/10.1080/15427587.2021.1935957.

21. Keoni Mahelona et al., "OpenAI's Whisper Is Another Case Study in Colonisation," Papa Reo, January 24, 2023, https://blog.papareo.nz/whisper-is-another-case-study-in-colonisation/.

22. Pierre Bourdieu, *Language and Symbolic Power* (Cambridge, MA: Harvard University Press, 1991).

23. Ethan Kutlu, "Now You See Me, Now You Mishear Me: Raciolinguistic Accounts of Speech Perception in Different English Varieties," *Journal of Multilingual and Multicultural Development* 44, no. 6 (2023): 511–525, https://doi.org/10.1080/01434632.2020.1835929.

24. Ryuko Kubota, "Critical Multiculturalism and Second Language Education," in *Critical Pedagogies and Language Learning*, ed. Bonny Norton and Kelleen Toohey (Cambridge: Cambridge University Press, 2004), 30–52, https://doi.org/10.1017/CBO9781139524834.003.

## Conclusion

1. Suzanne Gessner, Tracey Herbert, and Aliana Parker, *Report on the Status of B.C. First Nations Languages* (Brentwood Bay, BC: First Peoples' Cultural Council, 2022), https://fpcc.ca/wp-content/uploads/2023/02/FPCC-Language Report-23.02.14-FINAL.pdf.

2. Colleen M. Fitzgerald, "Understanding Language Vitality and Reclamation as Resilience: A Framework for Language Endangerment and 'Loss' (Commentary on Mufwene)," *Language* 93, no. 4 (2017): e280–e297, https://doi.org/10.1353/lan.2017.0072.

# FURTHER READING

Adamou, Evangelia. *The Adaptive Bilingual Mind: Insights from Endangered Languages*. Cambridge: Cambridge University Press, 2021.

Bowern, Claire. *Linguistic Fieldwork: A Practical Guide*. New York: Palgrave Macmillan, 2008.

Campbell, Lyle, and Anna Belew, eds. *Cataloguing the World's Endangered Languages*. London: Routledge, 2018.

Evans, Nicholas. *Words of Wonder: Endangered Languages and What They Tell Us*. Hoboken, NJ: Wiley, 2022.

Hinton, Leanne, Leena Huss, and Gerald Roche, eds. *The Routledge Handbook of Language Revitalization*. London: Routledge, 2018. https://doi.org/10.4324/9781315561271.

Leonard, Wesley Y. "Reflections on (De)Colonialism in Language Documentation." *Language Documentation and Conservation* 15 (2018): 55–65. http://hdl.handle.net/10125/24808.

Leonard, Wesley Y. "When Is an 'Extinct Language' Not Extinct? Miami, a Formerly Sleeping Language." In *Sustaining Linguistic Diversity: Endangered and Minority Languages and Language Varieties*, edited by Kendall A. King, Natalie Schilling-Estes, Jia Jackie Lou, Lyn Fogle, and Barbara Soukup, 23–34. Washington, DC: Georgetown University Press, 2008.

Leonard, Wesley Y., and Erin Haynes. "Making 'Collaboration' Collaborative: An Examination of Perspectives That Frame Linguistic Field Research." *Language Documentation and Conservation* 4 (2010): 269–293. http://hdl.handle.net/10125/4482.

Perley, Bernard C. "Zombie Linguistics: Experts, Endangered Languages and the Curse of Undead Voices." *Anthropological Forum* 22, no. 2 (2012): 133–149. https://doi.org/10.1080/00664677.2012.694170.

Seyfeddinipur, Mandana, Felix Ameka, Lissant Bolton, Jonathan Blumtritt, Brian Carpenter, Hilaria Cruz, Sebastian Drude, et al. "Public Access to Research Data in Language Documentation: Challenges and Possible Strategies,"

*Language Documentation and Conservation* 13 (2019): 545–563. http://hdl.handle.net/10125/24901.

Taff, Alice, Melvatha Chee, Jaeci Hall, Millie Yéi Dulitseen Hall, Kawenniyóhstha Nicole Martin, and Annie Johnston. "Indigenous Language Use Impacts Wellness." In *The Oxford Handbook of Endangered Languages*, edited by Kenneth L. Rehg and Lyle Campbell, 861–884. Oxford: Oxford University Press, 2018. https://doi.org/10.1093/oxfordhb/9780190610029.013.41.

Thomason, Sarah G. *Endangered Languages*. Cambridge: Cambridge University Press, 2015.

Woods, Lesley. *Something's Gotta Change: Redefining Collaborative Linguistic Research*. Canberra: Australian National University Press, 2023. https://doi.org/10.22459/SGC.2022.

# INDEX

**EVANGELIA ADAMOU** is Senior Researcher at the French National Centre for Scientific Research (CNRS) and a member of the Academy of Europe. She specializes in the study of endangered languages and has conducted extensive research in the Balkans and Latin America.